FOOD LOVERS'
GUIDE TO
PHILADELPHIA

Help Us Keep This Guide Up to Date

We would love to hear from you concerning your experiences with this guide and how you feel it could be improved and kept up to date. Please send your comments and suggestions to:

editorial@GlobePequot.com

Thanks for your input, and happy travels!

FOOD LOVERS' SERIES

FOOD LOVERS'
GUIDE TO
PHILADELPHIA

The Best Restaurants, Markets & Local Culinary Offerings

1st Edition

Iris McCarthy

Guilford, Connecticut

Editor: Amy Lyons
Project Editor: Lynn Zelem
Layout Artist: Mary Ballachino
Text Design: Sheryl Kober
Illustrations by Jill Butler with additional art by Carleen Moira Powell and MaryAnn Dubé
Base map provided by Compass Maps Ltd.
Map © Morris Book Publishing, LLC

ISBN 978-0-7627-7945-1

Printed in the United States of America

All the information in this guidebook is subject to change. We recommend that you call ahead to obtain current information before traveling.

Contents

Appendix: Eateries by Cuisine, 257

Index, 265

About the Author

Iris McCarthy is a food writer in the Greater Philadelphia region who has long held a passion for writing and food culture. Having spent nearly a decade in corporate America, she left to pursue her writing career full-time and hasn't looked back since. Currently, Iris pens articles for food columns of several local upscale lifestyle publications focused on telling the stories of the movers and shakers behind the region's lively culinary scene. In addition, she also contributes to a host of magazines, catalogs, and blogs.

Iris lives in the Philadelphia suburbs, but spends much of her time eating, working, and playing in the city. When she's not attending local food events, scoping out new ice cream spots to satiate her sweet tooth, or covering the Philly food scene, Iris can be found checking out the latest community theaters and museums.

Follow Iris as she dines around Philadelphia and the surrounding suburbs on her popular food blog **The Palate Princess** at the palateprincess.com and via Twitter @PalatePrincess.

Acknowledgments

First and foremost, I am grateful for the journey on which the pursuit of my passion has taken me and humble enough to realize that this book would not exist if it were not for the help of others.

I owe an infinite amount of gratitude to my mother, who spent countless hours listening to and reading the fantastical stories I penned in my adolescence. She liked to say that I was born with a pen in hand and would be tickled beyond belief to see my name in a byline or on a book cover.

To my father, I would like to thank you for teaching me that sometimes one has to kick down the door of opportunity instead of waiting for opportunity to make the first move. Your advice has served me well.

To those in my inner circle who have ridden the roller coaster with me and endured the full spectrum of my emotions during this process, I thank you. Dinner's on me.

To Amy Lyons of Globe Pequot Press, thank you for your support and patience and working tirelessly behind the scenes—all the while affording me the opportunity to do what I love.

To the readers of my blog The Palate Princess, I cannot thank you enough for helping me grow what started out as a hobby into a full-fledged career. Your continued readership, support, and comments mean so much to me.

Lastly and most importantly, I would like to extend the biggest thank you to the chefs, restaurateurs, waitstaff, farmers, and food artisans of the city of Philadelphia and its suburbs for doing what you do with such fiery passion and grace. You are the true gems of the city.

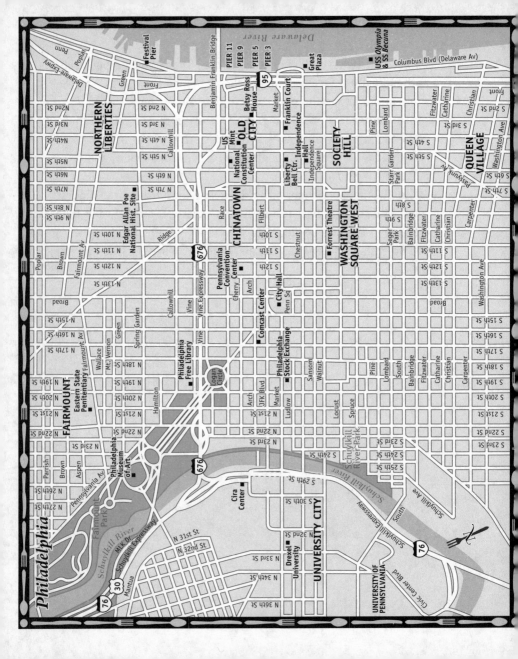

Introduction

Philadelphia is often thought of as a hardscrabble, scrappy city of hard knocks replete with citizens who would much rather devour scores of cheesesteaks and other handheld delights than pull up a chair at a white tablecloth, James Beard Award–winning fine dining establishment. Nothing could be further from the truth and, for the record, Philadelphia cuisine embodies much more than the cheesesteak. While the iconic foods normally associated with the city have their much deserved place in the annals of Philadelphia food history, the dining scene encompasses a mix of incomparable talent and several cuisines. Those with sophisticated, refined palates are just as comfortable dining in the city as those whose cravings rarely stretch beyond street food and takeout.

In terms of culinary history, Philadelphia's story is really no different from that of other major cities. In large part, it owes that rich history to both past and recent immigration. Ethnic groups from far and wide brought native foods and cooking techniques with them, leaving an indelible (and still visible) mark on the city. The geographical layout of the city was clearly drawn by ethnic lines—with territory names like Chinatown and the Italian Market, it was clear who lived where.

Most of South Philadelphia's communities are largely Italian-American. In the late 20th century, a sharp increase in immigration boosted the area's Vietnamese and Cambodian populations as well as its Russian and Mexican populations. Today, the term "Italian Market" is a bit of a misnomer as evidenced by the burgeoning number of Vietnamese and Thai restaurants and Asian and Mexican vendors interspersed with historic Italian ones. One could take a culinary trip around the world just by wandering from block to block—from steaming bowls of pho and the hoagie-like *bánh mì* to *al pastor* and Italian charcuterie, the diversity of the market serves as a testament to the heterogeneity of Philadelphia itself.

Certainly, there was a time when Philadelphia was an haute cuisine desert but in 1970, a young French chef named Georges Perrier came along and opened the now-legendary Le Bec-Fin and is credited with single-handedly ushering in the city's fine dining revolution. Never before had the city seen such technique and skill or grandiosity for that matter. Today, Philadelphia is home to renowned chefs like Marc Vetri, José Garces, Jeffrey Michaud, and Michael Solomonov. Even New York's Eric Ripert, chef-owner of Michelin-starred Le Bernardin has dipped his toe in the culinary waters of the city.

These chefs, along with a legion of their colleagues, are forging new paths in the culinary world while remaining true to their food philosophies and being mindful of seasonality and sustainability. Philadelphia is in the unique geographical position of being centrally located among major farmland and agricultural resources. Certainly, there are chefs who engage in a bit of "urban farming" with rooftop gardens and cultivate the occasional *potager,* but most chefs will cite their working relationships with local purveyors, farmers, and fishmongers as their most important ones. With chefs taking full advantage of these relationships and using fresh, local ingredients to create the most beautiful dishes of food, this is truly an exciting time in Philadelphia's dining history.

By no means is this book a directory; you will not find each and every Philadelphia establishment listed. The following pages are meant to serve as an insider's guide of sorts—showcasing the best of what the city has to offer. While it is important to give landmarks and the well-known their due, it is equally important to shine a light on those often hidden, untapped gems that reside on side streets and in less-frequented areas of the city.

Philadelphia: A History of Iconic Eats

Much like other large metropolises, the city of Philadelphia largely owes its diverse cuisine to the influx of immigrants during its formative years. They brought with them the food and cooking techniques of their homelands and some of those foodstuffs (or variations thereof) have come to represent the city itself and their depth and breadth stretch far beyond the perimeter of the typical foods most commonly associated with Philadelphia. Drink, more specifically alcohol, also played an important role in the shaping of the dining culture of the city. At the very least, the colonial affinity for spirits gave rise to the need for the construction of more taprooms—a few of which still stand today. As a hotbed of political activity, 18th-century Philadelphia saw a drastic increase in the number of city taverns and pubs that often doubled as meeting places for some of the men whose names would later grace  the Declaration of Independence. **City Tavern** (p. 66), the Old City landmark, was one such place. One of the city's most prominent tipplers, the venerable jack-of-all-trades Benjamin Franklin, once wrote that "there can't be good living where there is not good drinking" and, surprisingly, the favored modern-day libations of choice mimic those of colonial tavern favorites—beer and ale. Even though Philadelphians love to imbibe, make no mistake, Philadelphia is a food town.

When it comes to food, it should come as no surprise that Philadelphia is a real meat-and-potatoes kind of town or, more accurately, a *meat-and-bread* kind of town. It's no secret—no other city in the world adores the sandwich like Philly. Although there is debate as to the true date of its origin, the lauded cheesesteak is believed to have been invented in the 1930s. It is virtually a rule that all iconic foods must have a fantastical story attached to its origin and the cheesesteak is no different. As legend has it, brothers and hot dog vendors Harry and Pat Olivieri cemented their place in gastronomic history by stuffing a hot dog bun with sliced steak and giving it to a taxi driver. (Later, one of their cooks added melted cheese and essentially created the cheesesteak in its present-day form.) The 1930s family-owned hot dog stand eventually became south Philadelphia landmark **Pat's King of Steaks** (p. 117) which is still owned by the Olivieri family.

In a town that places the humble sandwich on a well-deserved pedestal, there is another kind of sandwich that enjoys a high ranking on the list of top Philadelphia foods. While it has a varying number of regional names like sub, submarine 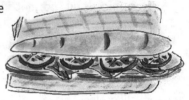 sandwich, grinder, or zep, any Philadelphian will tell you that within city limits, it is simply referred to as a hoagie. No doubt influenced by the heavy Italian-American presence in the city, the early 1900s saw the creation of the traditional hoagie. Although the cheesesteak is, by far, the most famous sandwich, the hoagie (typically made with Italian meats, cheese, a variety of toppings, seasonings, and oil) was declared the "official sandwich of Philadelphia" in 1992.

One cannot discuss the iconic foods of Philadelphia without mentioning the regional phenomena pork roll and scrapple. Created in the mid-1800s, the former is also known as Taylor ham and, although produced mainly in neighboring New Jersey, it has earned a place on most breakfast menus in the city as has the acquired-taste scrapple—a processed loaf made from an amalgamation of pork trimmings, scraps (hence the name), and seasonings.

Thick, dark, and rich, snapper soup is a Philadelphia delicacy made from turtles (not fish as many often incorrectly guess) and often drizzled with a bit of sherry. Now-defunct landmark Bookbinder's was once famous for its snapper soup; the bisque-like soup is not complete without a few oyster crackers bobbing on its surface. And, no, not just any crackers will do—only the spherical OTC-stamped (Original Trenton Cracker) kind will suffice.

Tomato pie, another icon that owes its roots to the predominantly Italian-American area of South Philadelphia, is a popular food that most closely resembles a—*gasp*—cheeseless pizza. While it sounds blasphemous to some, it is a delight to most city-dwellers. Never eaten hot, it is common to find individual squares or whole pies of the bread-and-sauce wonder being sold in local Italian bakery cases.

In keeping with the city's steadfast love of all things bread, nothing embodies Philadelphia street food more than the soft pretzel. True sticklers for accuracy are quick to argue that the pretzel was invented in Europe not Philadelphia; but in the early 1900s, German and Swiss German immigrants—who later became known as the Pennsylvania Dutch—opened a number of bakeries in and around the city, introducing the pretzel to the masses. The now-shuttered Federal Pretzel Baking Company of South Philadelphia was the first mass-production pretzel bakery in Philadelphia and virtually set the standard for what would become an iconic snack.

The torrid love affair with snacks doesn't stop there—hot-weather favorite water ice (yes, Philadelphians realize the redundancy), formally Italian ice, is often associated with Philadelphia, though it is not to be confused with shaved ice. True Italian ice is made in the same manner as ice cream by simultaneously freezing and mixing ice and flavoring or fresh ingredients. Beloved city staples **Italiano's** (p. 24) in South Philadelphia and **John's Water Ice** (p. 24) in the Italian Market section of the city are renowned for their authenticity.

Another seasonal treat, the spiced wafer—specifically those made by the Pennsylvania-based company Sweetzels—is anxiously anticipated in the cooler months. The spicy wafers are a variation of the colonial-era ginger and molasses cookie and can be found in local grocery stores and scooped up by the boxful when available. Perhaps more beloved than water ice and the spiced wafer combined is the regional confection known as the Krimpet, a buttery snack cake topped with a layer of butterscotch icing, manufactured by Philadelphia's own Tasty Baking Company (more commonly known by its brand name Tastykake). In 2010, Tastykake announced the imminent sale of its baking facility, which caused such an outpouring of protests from city residents that the sale was halted—proving just how nostalgic and serious Philadelphians are about our food.

While not typically associated with the area, another popular sweet treat was birthed in the city. Much to the chagrin of dentists everywhere and further affirming Philadelphia's affinity for the

How to "Speak Philly"

"What accent?" That's the reply you're likely to receive if you question a Philadelphian about his manner of speaking. While not as nasal as a Midwestern accent or quite as strong as, say, a Boston accent, there's a definite "sound" that separates Philadelphia from the rest. The Philly accent is as distinct as that of residents in the neighboring states of New Jersey and New York and bears a strong resemblance to both. Perhaps there is no better time to experience the unique coupling of the accent and phraseology than when ordering food at a Philadelphia eatery. Below is a guide to help you decode the local dialect and navigate your way through the ordering process:

"Didjaeatyet?" "Did you eat yet?" is the official motto of famed sandwich hotspot **Paesano's** (p. 8)—it's even emblazoned on the staff's t-shirts. Asking someone if he has eaten yet is almost a kind of greeting and akin to asking "How are you?" In the city that's always hungry, you're bound to hear this one a lot. As a variation, expect to hear "You's eat?" as well—"you's" being a totally acceptable substitution for the more proper "you."

"Witterwitout?" "With or without?" is a common question when ordering the venerable cheesesteak. Often times, vendors forgo pleasantries and instead opt for speeding up the ordering process by getting right to the point. Be prepared to answer properly by knowing the tried-and-true response (see below).

"Whiz wit/wit'out" These two all-important cheesesteak ordering methods could mean the difference between sniffed out as a tourist or being respected as a local. To order a "whiz wit" means you want your steak topped with Cheez Whiz and fried onions; a "wit'out" is made— you guessed it—without the onions. Just about every cheesesteak vendor in town recognizes the ordering lingo and is happy to serve those in the know. Remember, this is a city where the cheesesteak is a civic symbol and an icon, so it's a good idea to get the lingo down pat before setting foot in a line because asking, "May I have a cheesesteak sandwich with fried onions?" is sheer sacrilege and the love shown to those who get it wrong can be—well, a little less than *brotherly*.

"Wooder ice" Grammar lovers beware! The bastardization of the word "water" is commonplace—especially in South Philly. Philadelphians are already aware that the term "water ice" sounds strange to out-of-towners who call it Italian ice, so do yourself a favor and don't point that out—just enjoy the sound of the sometimes hilarious Philadelphia pronunciation and accent.

"Philadelphia Iggles" First things first, the Philadelphia Eagles are an NFL team—they are not edible—but the team is worth mentioning because talking about food and one's favorite sports team often goes hand in hand. For example, one might say, "Yo, I just watched the Iggles get crushed—I need a whiz wit bad." *Translation:* "The Philadelphia Eagles just suffered another crushing defeat and, to nurse my wounds, I am in desperate need of a cheesesteak with Cheez Whiz and fried onions." Much more fun to say it the Philly way, right?

"Beggles" Yes, Philadelphians love bagels almost as much as New Yorkers and we have some pretty awesome bagel joints to prove it. In the city, the word "bagel" gets the same dialect treatment as "eagles" (see above).

"Pressels/prezzels" Ahh, pretzels—Philadelphia's street snack of choice. If you're in line and hear someone ordering a *pressel* or *prezzel,* you don't need a GPS to tell you you're most likely in a South Philly neighborhood.

sugary stuff, soda pop was invented in the early 1800s by local pharmacist Townsend Speakman by combining fruit-infused syrup and carbonated water. (Philadelphians John Hart and Dr. Phillip Syng Physick are credited with inventing carbonated water.) Today, a line of Physick's original recipe sodas are sold in local specialty grocery stores; history buffs will be pleased to find them being sold at the Historic Philadelphia Center in Old City.

Organization

The guide is divided into four main geographic sections—North, Northeast & Northwest; Center City; South & Southwest; and West—with individual neighborhoods and communities listed at the beginning of each chapter for easy reference. To further clarify, each establishment is listed alphabetically along with its address and neighborhood.

Following the main geographic chapters are special regional gastronomic chapters called Sips & the City, Farm Fresh, Suburban Gems, and Festivals & Events.

North, Northeast & Northwest

Avenue of the Arts North, Chestnut Hill, East Falls, Fairmount, Far Northeast, Francisville, Hunting Park, Logan, Market East, Midtown Village, Northern Liberties, North Philadelphia, Oxford Circle, Roxborough/Manayunk, Spring Garden, Fishtown, Kensington, Port Richmond

Center City

Art Museum District, Avenue of the Arts, Chinatown, Logan Square, Market East, Midtown Village, Old City, Penn Center, Rittenhouse Square, Society Hill, South Street District, Washington Square West

South & Southwest

Angora, Bella Vista, Graduate Hospital, Grays Ferry, Italian Market, Newbold, Pennsport, Point Breeze, Queen Village, South Philadelphia, Southwark, Southwest Philadelphia

West

University City, Walnut Hill, West Philadelphia

Sips & the City

This section profiles where the city's best watering holes—both dive and upscale—along with popular wine bars can be found.

Farm Fresh

There are plenty of places in Philadelphia that bring the country to the city. A host of farmers' markets, CSAs, and food share programs can be found in this section.

Suburban Gems

While this book deals primarily with establishments located within city limits, the crop of notable eateries that lie on the outskirts of Philadelphia should not be missed. Also featured here is a delectable ice cream tour, an overview of the bounty surrounding Philadelphia, and a list of the top suburban culinary classes.

Festivals & Events

Philadelphia is undeniably a fun city and many of its festivals and events are food-centric. While there is always something going on, an annual calendar of events is listed in the book.

Recipes

Some of the city's top chefs have lifted the veil on their best recipes and shared them on these pages.

How to Use This Book

First and foremost, this book is not meant to be an exhaustive directory—you will find only the best of Philadelphia in these pages. Information on restaurants, landmark eateries, gourmet specialty shops, and farmers markets is provided as well as informative sidebars that highlight notable eats, hotspots, and interesting tidbits.

Price Code

Each listing includes one to four dollar signs indicating a general pricing guide. The pricing guide indicates the approximate cost per person for a meal including one drink, tax, and tip.

$	**Thrifty, $10 and under**
$$	**Moderate, $10 to $30**
$$$	**Expensive, $30 to $60**
$$$$	**Splurge, $60 and above**

Landmarks

Long-standing establishments that have not only changed the dining landscape of Philadelphia but also contributed something significant to the city's food culture are listed in this section.

Foodie Faves

As the title implies, this section will list local restaurants based on general popularity. Whether for a signature dish or an all-around great meal, only the notable make the cut.

Post-Midnight Munching

Thankfully, there are a number of establishments that cater to the set who realize hunger can't be confined to standard operating hours. Many late-night eateries keep their kitchens going until 1 a.m. or later and there are plenty of places that will help you satisfy your nighttime cravings. These establishments can be found in each section of the book.

Specialty Stores, Markets & Producers

Philadelphia is a great city for specialty shopping. While most of the entries listed offer local goods, there are some that offer hard-to-find imported goods. The local farmers' markets are also a thing of beauty—with plenty of year-round markets dotted throughout the city. Several city wineries offer local labels as well.

Culinary Classes & Food Tours

There are several opportunities to learn more about food and drink in Philadelphia—from interactive cooking classes to beer and wine instruction at local wine bars to private cheese classes. There are also a number of food tours in the city and surrounding countryside that get participants out of the kitchen and into the streets for up close and personal contact with local resources.

Keeping Up with Food News

In the past few years, the Philadelphia food writing and blogging scene has exploded. There are a number of local publications that dedicate substantial ink to exploring food news and food culture while managing to establish clear—sometimes quirky, tongue-in-cheek—voices that keep the public informed about everything from food events and restaurant openings to highlighting area chefs. Food bloggers have proven themselves to be a sort of league of citizen journalists with many blogs going beyond simply sharing recipes and cooking tips by delving into and tackling real issues and capturing impressive and poignant images of the Philadelphia food scene through beautiful photography. Here are some local publications and bloggers that have their fingers on the pulse of the city's culinary scene:

Eater, eater.com/Philadelphia. Eater has several editions in various cities; the Philadelphia edition covers all food-related news, gossip, and tidbits. This is definitely a site to bookmark if you're looking for up-to-the-minute coverage of restaurant openings and interesting reads on local chefs.

foobooz, foobooz.com. Started by Arthur Etchells in 2006, the site that began as a hobby has grown to become the leading authority on all things culinary in the city of Philadelphia; it was purchased by *Philadelphia* magazine in 2010. If it happens within city limits, the staff at foobooz is likely in the know. The site manages to get the scoop on restaurant openings, closings, up-and-coming chefs, and kitchen gossip, which all makes for exciting reading indeed.

Food in Jars, foodinjars.com. Blogger, author, and all-around local foodie celebrity Marisa McClellan captivates audiences with

her vast knowledge of canning and preserving an array of foods. While her blog focuses on highlighting a method of food preservation that harks back to a simpler time, Marisa is doing some positively innovative things with—well, food in jars. From root vegetable pickles to blood-orange marmalade, the in-depth and instructional blog showcases the art of "putting up" using local produce.

Fussing with Forks, fussingwithforks.com. A self-described part-time foodie and full-time photographer, Jason Varney is one of Philadelphia's most prominent food photographers. If you've flipped through the pages of a local glossy and spotted a food picture that made you salivate, chances are you were staring at a Jason Varney photo. His gorgeous photography and ability to elevate food through pictures makes him a sought-after photographer by restaurateurs and magazine editors alike.

Holly Eats, hollyeats.com. Hollister "Holly" Moore is quite the man about town—actually, he's a man about a lot of towns. The whole premise of the former restaurateur's well-read blog is finding the best and cheapest eats all over the country. His home base, or "chomping ground" as he puts it, is Philadelphia, and if a place serves great food at a great price, Holly is sure to write about it and give it a high ranking on his grease stain rating system.

Madame Fromage, madamefromage.blogspot.com. Learning the subtleties and nuances of cheese is as daunting a task as learning about wine, but blogger and cheese enthusiast Tenaya Darlington lifts the veil on the art of cheese tasting with her informative blog. She hails from—where else—Wisconsin, and moved to Philadelphia in 2005. Today, she teaches fun, interactive cheese classes and hosts private tastings. From the mild to the stinky, Madame Fromage is the definitive blog for any cheese lover.

Meal Ticket, citypaper.net/blogs/mealticket. Meal Ticket is a City Paper blog about food, food news, the local dining scene and a host of random food-related items. The staff and the paper's contributors are a quirky hybrid of wordsmiths and food lovers with a penchant for tongue-in-cheek, irreverent writing. The well-read blog high-lights the staff's own kitchen successes (and failures), restaurants, interviews, and personal commentary on all things food.

Midtown Lunch, midtownlunch.com/Philadelphia. The employed know how precious those 30 to 60 minutes known as the lunch break really are. So do the folks at Midtown Lunch, so they created a site that is devoted to finding good lunchtime eats at great prices (under $10). The site originally focused on Manhattan but eventually expanded to other markets. The Philadelphia edition is the go-to site for discovering cheap eats in the city.

Penn Appétit, pennappetit.blogspot.com. *Penn Appétit* is the University of Pennsylvania's award-winning student-run food magazine. Don't equate this endeavor with a typical boring school newspaper—the innovative UPenn students publish a polished, well-written hardcover magazine once a semester and curate a blog that is updated daily with restaurant reviews, food news, and musings.

22nd & Philly, 22ndandphilly.com. This informative blog is written by Bradd and Kristy—two Center City professionals who profess to be nothing more than lovers of great food. Their unpretentious accounts of the Philadelphia dining scene are well written and thorough; don't miss the pair's frequent guides that offer mini-compilations of the best Philadelphia has to offer.

Uwishunu, uwishunu.com. Described as Philadelphia's go-to dining, entertainment and leisure travel guide, uwishunu is the official blog of the Greater Philadelphia Tourism Marketing Corporation and focuses on the best of the city. The blog does an excellent job of keeping up with what's going on in the city and the suburbs.

Culinary Classes & Food Tours

In addition to these offerings, see the listings that begin on p. 106.

City Food Tours, Chinatown; (800) 979-3370; cityfoodtours .com. If you've ever wanted a true Philly food experience, this is the tour for you. City Food Tours takes participants off the tour-  isty beaten path and offers them the chance to eat like locals while visiting some of the city's tastiest places. Sampling mouthwatering food and drink like cheesesteaks and craft beer and noshing on snacks like soft pretzels and fine chocolates are part of the package on this outing. The informative walking tours are led by local food experts who love nothing more than pulling back the curtain on the city's best eats and sharing insider's tips on how foods are made. The 2- to 3-hour excursions include public tours like "Flavors of Philly," "Decadent Gourmet," "Ethnic Eats," and the recently added "Taste of Northern Liberties"—a jaunt through one of the city's trendiest neighbor-hoods. Youngsters can also get in on the fun; private kiddie tours can be arranged for budding foodies. The tours are offered year-round and the meeting spots vary; check the website for specifics.

COOK, Rittenhouse Square, 253 S. 20th St., Philadelphia, PA 19103; (215) 735-2665; audreyclairecook.com. It's extremely dif-ficult to pigeonhole COOK into a single category—the Rittenhouse Square space is a hybrid mix of bookstore, boutique, classroom, and kitchen. The 16-seat kitchen classroom, the brainchild of local restaurateur Audrey Claire Taichman, hosts a variety of decorated local culinary masters who teach classes on topics ranging from gluten-free gourmet to *sous vide* cooking. The hefty schedule offers a number of classes each month and even though they are not cheap—they typically range from $80–$185—they consistently sell out. Check the website for an updated list of classes and book early.

Fante's Kitchen Shop, Italian Market, 1006 S. 9th St., Philadelphia, PA 19147; (215) 922-5557; fantes.com. Opened in 1906, Fante's claims to be the oldest cookware shop in the nation and, ironically, it is one of the few remaining Italian vendors in the Italian Market. Wandering through the stocked-to-the-rafters aisles is like going on a treasure hunt and will uncover obscure kitchen utensils, gadgets, accessories, and a host of baking supplies. High-end brand name items like beautiful enameled Le Creuset cookware and Mauviel copper pots are usually wallet draining when purchased from larger competitors, but a cookware enthusiast could conceivably shop at this boutique establishment without breaking the bank. Don't quite know what that odd-looking gadget is in Aisle Two? Most of the staff members are cooks and bakers and are always willing to demonstrate and explain—often making the shopping experience an informative and fun lesson.

Philadelphia's Iconic Eats: Where to Find 'Em

Finding the best of some of Philly's iconic eats can be a daunting task. Here's a list of the best places to discover a few legendary eats. Be sure to see the "How to 'Speak Philly'" sidebar on p. 8 for tips on ordering!

Cheesesteaks

For years, a sometimes contentious battle has been waged between two of the city's most iconic landmarks. Admittedly, **Geno's Steaks** (p. 116) and **Pat's King of Steaks** (p. 117) have become too touristy for many native Philadelphians but the undeniable fact remains that both long-standing establishments have engrained themselves in the city's culinary topography by serving distinctly different cheesesteaks— the former serving sliced rib eye and the latter opting to serve its rib eye chopped. It is not an exaggeration—marriages have been tested and whole families have been divided over the sliced/chopped debate. **Jim's Steaks** (*multiple locations;* 400 South St., Philadelphia, PA 19147; jimssteaks.com; 215-928-1911) is also one of the most popular cheesesteak joints in the city and even though on most days there's a line of eager patrons snaked around the building, Jim's has somehow managed to avoid being branded a tourist trap of Geno's and Pat's proportions. Speaking of branding, the cheesesteaks are often thought to be the best in the city.

Roast Pork Sandwiches

While the venerated cheesesteak garners most of the sandwich fame, it's a little-known fact that it is not the official sandwich of Philadelphia. In fact, there are some locals who wince at the association of the city with the cheesesteak and consider the roast pork sandwich more authentically Philly. Perhaps there's no more famous roast pork sandwich crafter than Tony Luke Jr. Most non-Philadelphians became acquainted with the restaurateur when he defeated TV superstar chef Bobby Flay in a roast pork throwdown. His eponymous eatery, **Tony Luke's** (*multiple locations*; 39 E. Oregon Ave., Philadelphia, PA 19148; tonylukes.com; 215-551-5725), has become one of the top sandwich destinations in the city and, even though the hoagies and cheesesteaks are wildly popular, it's the legendary roast pork sandwich with broccoli rabe and sharp provolone that draws the biggest crowds. Like all good sandwich shops in the city, James Beard Award–winning **John's Roast Pork** (14 Snyder Ave., Philadelphia, PA 19148; johnsroastpork.com; 215-463-1951) offers a varied menu but, as the name implies, special-

izes in juicy roast pork sandwiches. (Another noteworthy specialty is a bacon and Cheez Whiz–loaded hot dog known as the Texas Tommy.) For the bravehearted willing to withstand an endless line and the madness of bustling Reading Terminal Market, **Tommy DiNic's** (1136 Arch St., Philadelphia, PA 19147; 215-923-6175) is a must. Specializing in heaping, drool-worthy sandwiches, the juicy roast pork sandwich is a thing of wonder. To get the true experience, top it off with sharp provolone and broccoli rabe; your mouth will thank you.

Soft Pretzels

Philadelphia adopted the European twisted treat long ago and it is still a favorite on city streets and in mom-and-pop shops dotted all over town. If you should find yourself needing a boost of energy in the form of a carb-laden snack, **Miller's Twist** (51 N. 12th St., Philadelphia, PA 19107; millerstwist.com; 717-669-6409) in Reading Terminal Market offers a variety of buttery, slightly salty Amish-style pretzels; traditional twists and sticks and a host of pretzel dogs are available. For the pretzel purists, **Philly Soft Pretzel Company** (*multiple locations*; 1532 Sansom St., Philadelphia, PA 19195; phillysoftpretzelfactory.com; 215-569-3988) serves up traditional pretzels in all their wheat-y goodness fresh out of the oven. Chewy and slightly doughy, pretzels from this bakery chain are generally thought to be the real deal. Speaking of real deals, **Center City Pretzel Company** (816 Washington Ave., Philadelphia, PA 19147; 215-463-5664) is an authentic pretzel bakery specializing in traditional Philly pretzels only. You'll find no pretzel dogs, pretzel bites, or fancy mustards at this late-night hotspot—just amazing old-fashioned pretzels crafted in true Philly style. Those in the know make sure to arrive just after the place opens at midnight to get their hands on the first batch out of the oven and, at a mere 35 cents apiece, you can afford to satisfy your inner pretzel glutton.

Water Ice

Just about everywhere else, the sweet treat is called Italian ice but in Philadelphia it's known as water ice. Although out-of-towners snicker at Philadelphians' choice to call it such, who cares about the moniker when it tastes so good? **John's Water Ice** (701 Christian St., Philadelphia, PA 19147; 215-925-6955; johnswaterice.com) is a hometown favorite that serves up some of the city's best water ice, gelati, and ice cream. Water ice flavors are limited to lemon, cherry, pineapple, and chocolate but patrons hardly seem to mind because John's has been consistently dishing out high-quality water ice for so many years that expanding the flavor list would seem a bit like gilding the lily. **Pop's Homemade Water Ice** (1337 W. Oregon Ave., Philadelphia, PA 19176; 215-551-7677) has earned the reputation of being *the* place to grab a "wooder ice" (see "How to 'Speak Philly,'" p. 8) pre- or post-Phillies game. Here, the icy stuff is made with real chunks of fruit pieces and Pop's even goes so far as to dip its toe in the adventurous waters with the banana split water ice—banana water ice, mini chocolate chips, and maraschino cherries. Those looking to appease their inner "kid in a candy store" will appreciate the hard and soft-serve ice cream selection, frozen bananas and soft pretzels served "wiz wit" or "wit'out" (see "How to 'Speak Philly,'" p. 8), but really nothing holds a candle to the water ice. Regarded as the hands-down best water ice in the entire city, **Italiano's** (2551 S. 12th St., Philadelphia, PA 19148; 215-465-1780) takes credit for inventing the popular gelati—unique sweet treats made by alternating layers of water ice and soft-serve ice cream. While Italiano's definitely oozes a South Philly vibe, the water ice flavors easily cater to a more sophisticated palate and those seeking to explore beyond scoops of cherry and lemon. Mind-blowing concoctions like ginger ale and amaretto sound simplistic but are a surprising revelation; sweet seekers everywhere must put this place in their repertoire.

North, Northeast & Northwest Philadelphia

Avenue of the Arts North, Chestnut Hill, East Falls, Fairmount, Far Northeast, Francisville, Hunting Park, Logan, Market East, Midtown Village, Northern Liberties, North Philadelphia, Oxford Circle, Roxborough/Manayunk, Spring Garden, Fishtown, Kensington, Port Richmond

With its landscape scarred by abandoned warehouses and dilapidated historic buildings whose former glory days are long gone, North Philadelphia has earned a reputation as a hardscrabble, hard knocks section of the city. In the not-so-distant past, the mere mention of the area becoming a power player on the Philadelphia dining scene would have garnered a fair share of scoffs but today some notable eateries are beginning to emerge thanks, in part, to chefs like Marc Vetri and restaurateurs like Stephen Starr.

Known largely for its takeout spots, pizzerias, and greasy spoons, the area has hidden gems that true food enthusiasts know how to sniff out, from brunch spots to delis to sushi eateries. Those in the know head to the Roxborough/Manayunk area which is home to some of the city's best watering holes—after all, the name Manayunk is derived from a Lenni Lenape Indian word meaning "where we go to drink." Having undergone a fairly recent revitalization, Northern Liberties has become a dining destination of the upwardly mobile and trendy 20- and 30-something sets with its burger joints, tapas restaurants, and cafes. A quick jaunt to restaurant-laden Germantown Avenue will put you smack dab in the middle of quaint Chestnut Hill's burgeoning culinary scene, where new restaurants crop up fairly frequently. Past reputation aside, North Philadelphia and its surrounding communities should be kept on your culinary radar.

Landmark

Winnie's LeBus, Roxborough/Manayunk; 4266 Main St., Philadelphia, PA 19127; (215) 487-2663; lebusmanayunk.com; Traditional American; $$. Long before the food truck revolution, LeBus was serving healthy comfort food from a yellow school bus on the campus of University of Pennsylvania. For over 25 years, homemade soups, good-for-you salads and homey favorites have been feeding the hungry masses. The breads baked in-house have made this landmark a regional household name with many area restaurants boasting LeBus breads and baked goods on their own menus. Lighter fare like the brown rice nut salad with a variety of nuts and seeds, kalamata olives, and feta are on par with heartier dishes like the popular "Mom's meatloaf." Stop by the in-house market where a selection of fresh homemade cupcakes, granola soups, salads, and—of course—their famous bread is sold. Large platters of prepared food from the menu are available; call ahead to order.

Foodie Faves

Agiato, Roxborough/Manayunk; 4359 Main St., Philadelphia, PA 19127; (215) 482-9700; agiatophila.com; Italian; $$. A spin-off of the Agiato Bread Company and modeled after European *paninotecas* and *enotecas,* Agiato offers a little slice of *la dolce vita* to the neighborhood of Manayunk. Exuding a casual and relaxed vibe, the cafe itself is outfitted with a large communal table and evokes the feeling of a family dinner; outdoor seating offers a view of the often busy main drag. Weekend brunch is an ideal morning starter; lunch and dinner menus include a selection of cured meats, cheeses, and crostini meant for sharing and a pretty broad panini offering. The *prosciutto cotto* and gruyère panino capped off with a lace-edged fried egg—essentially a tricked out ham and cheese sandwich—is the essence of a good lunch. If salads are what you seek, here they are simply prepared but complex in flavor—a duck confit, goat cheese, and dried cherry salad is a wise choice. A wine list and local beer roster attract oenophiles and hops heads alike.

Alex's Pizzeria, Roxborough/Manayunk; 400 Leverington Ave., Philadelphia, PA 19128; (215) 483-6126; Italian/Pizzeria; $. Pizza is one of the most hotly debated foods in the world, but any true pizza lover will acknowledge that the crust and sauce are the two most important elements of any pizza and it just so happens that Alex's Pizzeria does both extremely well. The small pizza parlor has been a neighborhood staple for years and serves a variety of pies and toppings and, for those looking to step outside of the traditional arena, there's a specialty pizza menu as well. The pies tend to run on the smallish side, so ordering a large pizza isn't as gluttonous as it sounds. Cash only.

Bar Ferdinand, Northern Liberties; 1030 N. 2nd St., Philadelphia, PA 19123; (215) 923-1313; barferdinand.com; Spanish; $$. Liberties Walk is home to a number of hipster hangouts and, since its revitalization, has become a sort of mecca for the young and trendy. Spanish tapas restaurant Bar Ferdinand specializes in authentic small plates and cocktails and is to the neighborhood of Northern

Liberties what rival tapas eatery **Amada** (p. 70) is to Old City—a stylish, sophisticated establishment with a sizable selection of mouthwatering dishes. The hot and cold tapas are impressive, but  the *croquetas*—a mixture of vegetables, fish, or meat rolled in breadcrumbs and fried—are the real draw. More than 50 authentic, hand-picked Spanish vinos grace the wine list so there is no lack of variety in choosing one that perfectly complements any of the tapas on the extensive menu.

Cafe Estelle, Northern Liberties; 444 N. 4th St., Philadelphia, PA 19123; (215) 925-5080; cafeestelle.com; Traditional American; $$. Long thought pretentious and a meal to be enjoyed only by those who sip from a teacup with a pinky in the air, brunch has reintroduced itself as a more approachable and accessible meal and gained a legion of loyal devotees—particularly the cool, hipster set who frequent the trendy Northern Liberties area. Cafe Estelle is lauded as one of the city's premier brunch spots—having won over diners by offering a tasty alternative to the classics like a breakfast pizza topped with home fries, provolone, house-made pancetta, and fried eggs. Breakfast and an array of soups and sandwiches round out the menu and, while you can't really go wrong with any of the offerings, missing brunch would be an unforgivable transgression.

Cafe Lift, Fairmount; 428 N. 13th St., Philadelphia, PA 19123; (215) 922-3031; cafelift.com; New American; $$. Set in a lofty brownstone in the old warehouse district, Cafe Lift attracts the young and trendy neighborhood crowd. The menu is as eclectic as the patrons who frequent this north Philadelphia eatery. For breakfast or lunch, enjoy a *crespelle,* an Italian-style crepe, stuffed with fresh sweet or savory ingredients or a variety of hot off the griddle panini. The outrageously creative menu has garnered serious fans who sing the praises of dishes like the cannoli french toast and the lemon-ricotta pancakes. In a city that places brunch on a very high pedestal, Cafe Lift is deserving of the accolades. Cash only.

Cantina dos Segundos, Northern Liberties; 931 N. 2nd St., Philadelphia, PA 19123; (215) 629-0500; cantinadossegundos.com; Mexican; $$. Seeking out decent Mexican food in this section of the city may prove as fruitful as the adventures of Don Quixote. This raucous Northern Liberties taqueria serves up tasty Mexican-American grub of Flintstone-ian proportions and the dishes can be made vegan or vegetarian—much to the delight of the noncarnivorous masses. Platters of *al pastor* burritos and tacos are large enough to share and an impressive list of tequilas and a rainbow of margarita flavors inspire the kind of lazy lounging that the late-night crowd adores.

Chabaa Thai Bistro, Manayunk; 4371 Main St., Philadelphia, PA 19127; (215) 483-1979; chabaathai.com; Thai; $$. To some Philadelphians, "suburbs" is the equivalent of a 4-letter word and, oftentimes, the thought of venturing outside the city center for a meal is inconceivable. Judging from the crowds who flock to the neighborhood of Manayunk seeking superbly done standards like Panang curry and pineapple jasmine fried rice, Chabaa Thai may be the exception to the rule. Large, fresh shrimp get bathed in a flavorful green curry and the crispy duck pad thai is a standout. Vegetarians and meat eaters alike can appreciate Chabaa's offerings where tofu-studded Thai basil rice comfortably shares menu space with *sai grog*—a lemongrass-infused pork appetizer. Typical in many Thai eateries, the menu employs a "heat dial" ordering practice— numbering a dish's heat factor from 1 to 3, although the promise of even the spiciest level won't be intimidating or unbearable to amateur heatseekers. See recipe for Chef Moon Krapugthong's **Thai Egg Custard** on p. 246.

Chubby's Cheesesteaks, Roxborough/Manayunk; 5826 Henry Ave., Philadelphia, PA 19128; (215) 487-2575; Traditional American/ Sandwiches; $. There are some things that are never documented in a history book and the fierce cheesesteak wars that have been brewing in the city for decades are among them. The fiercest of them all, by far, is the long-standing war waged between Geno's Steaks and Pat's. Lesser known, but no less intense, is the sandwich war between Dalessandro's and Chubby's. While Dalessandro's enjoys greater name recognition, to count Chubby's out as a serious sandwich contender is a grave mistake. The Roxborough sandwich shop consistently churns out quality food—with its cheesesteak and hoagie offerings ranking among the city's favorites. For the serious condiment connoisseur, the pickle and pepper bar is a nice touch and presents some delicious sandwich toppers.

The Couch Tomato Cafe, Roxborough/Manayunk; 102 Rector St., Philadelphia, PA 19127; (215) 483-2233; thecouchtomato.com; Italian/Pizza; $. This health-conscious, vegetarian-friendly pizzeria's claim to fame is its use of fresh ingredients and its assortment of homemade salad dressings. The enormous 20-inch pies are crafted using white or wheat crispy thin crusts and can be embellished with, in addition to standard toppings, thinking-outside-the-pizza-box surprises like fresh cilantro, roasted red potatoes, smoked Gouda or barbecued pork. If you're averse to carbs, fully customizable salads are a great choice and, like their pizza counterparts, can be made with a variety of toppings. There's also a rotating menu of homemade desserts.

Dalessandro's Steaks, Roxborough/Manayunk; 600 Wendover St., Philadelphia, PA 19128; (215) 482-5407; dalessandros.com; Traditional American/Sandwiches; $. Many people often mull over what their last meal would be if they knew their earthly exit was imminent and Dalessandro's usually ends up on the culinary wish list of many Philadelphians. In the City of Brotherly Love, the cheesesteak is a food group unto itself and just about everyone has an opinion on how to create a proper one. Dalessandro's, a classic Philly sandwich shop, has been a favorite for years—having perfectly mastered the all-important provolone-to-meat and whiz-to-meat ratios. (For those unfamiliar with cheesesteak talk, "whiz" refers to Cheez Whiz—that notorious neon orange liquid cheese whose use is generally frowned upon on anything other than a cheesesteak or fries.)

Dattilo's Delicatessen, Far Northeast; 8000 Horrocks St., Philadelphia, PA 19152; (215) 725-2020; dattilosdeli.com; Traditional American/Deli; $. Dattilo's is one of those places that seems like it's been around since the first brick of the neighborhood was laid; it's practically a landmark. You'll find a standard deli menu—hoagies, hot and cold sandwiches (the homemade meatball sandwich is praised as one of the best in the city and, considering Philadelphia's heavy Italian presence, that is a compliment not to be taken lightly), and a variety of cheesesteaks. While the menu may offer standard fare, don't count Dattilo's out as a one-trick pony; the eatery also has a fresh meat market and a catering facility for those who want to enjoy traditional deli eats at home.

Deke's BBQ, Roxborough/Manayunk; 443 Shurs Ln., Philadelphia, PA 19128; (215) 588-7427; dekesbar-b-que.com; Barbecue; $$. Discovering the taste of the South is no easy feat this side of the Mason-Dixon Line, but Deke's manages to coax out the slow, rich flavors for which barbecue is famous. You'll find a roundup of ribs, chicken, pulled pork, and brisket along with authentic sides like collard greens and gooey mac and cheese on the menu. The cocktails—or "newfangled adult beverages" as they are known at Deke's—are not to be missed and the fact that they are served in handled Mason jars just adds to the place's charm. If you're not too stuffed from the barbecue platters or too tipsy from imbibing, try a traditional Southern dessert like pecan pie or banana pudding.

Doma, Fairmount; 1822 Callowhill St., Philadelphia, PA 19130; (215) 564-1114; domarestaurant.com; Japanese; $$. Certainly, those seeking tamer offerings will find the California and spicy tuna rolls comforting, but Doma puts its best foot forward with its often daring, unusual combinations like the bibimbap roll which mimics the taste of the Korean dish after which it is modeled. Ordering individual pieces of sushi and rolls can get pricey so try opting for the sushi-sashimi *omakase* that features a substantial and varied selection of the day's freshest catch and is hand chosen by the chef. Pleasantly depart from the sushi-centric menu with a bowl of udon topped with a poached egg and shrimp tempura. Smaller appetites are happily satiated by well-prepared smaller bites like rock shrimp tempura and the insanely delicious steamed buns; the tuna-stuffed jalapeño deserves an honorable mention as well.

Fiorino, East Falls; 3572 Indian Queen Ln., Philadelphia, PA 19129; (215) 843-1500; fiorino.us; Italian; $$. Service can be a little disjointed and aloof at this Italian BYOB, but that doesn't discourage diners from squeezing into the tiny, 11-table dining room. They're most likely excited that restaurateur and veteran chef

Franco Faggi has decided to cross the river to East Falls and set up shop in a neighborhood whose dining scene has been rocky to say the least. The rustic menu is largely composed of comforting classics—a generous antipasto, salads, a limited offering of soups, pastas, meat entrees, and fish. A potato gnocchi so light you half expect it to rise from its swathing of creamy Gorgonzola sauce and a fresh, simply prepared tuna carpaccio with briny capers, olive oil, and a squeeze of fresh lemon are arguably the most notable plates.

A Full Plate, Northern Liberties; 1009 N. Bodine St., Philadelphia, PA 19176; (215) 627-4068; afullplate.net; New American; $$. The menu at this down home Northern Liberties BYO is as eclectic as the decor. The Southern-accented menu is a heady trip that consists of favorites like po' boys with tangy remoulade, heaping sandwiches and a rainbow of tasty sides—with both non-vegan and vegan options offered. The restaurant shines with its impressive brunch— chicken and waffles with barbecue syrup, crab Benedict, and the granola-crusted french toast are great choices as is a Southern ode to traditional huevos rancheros—an andouille sausage–studded delight served with red beans and rice and a sunny-side-up egg.

Green Eggs Cafe, Northern Liberties; 719 N. 2nd St., Philadelphia, PA 19123; (215) 922-3447; Traditional American; $$. Dr. Seuss may not have liked green eggs but Philadelphians sure do—well, not actual green eggs but rather Green Eggs Cafe. This is the kind of place you bring a group of friends for brunch—friends that don't mind you swiping a bite or two (or three) off their plates. The menu is large and there are always a few specials running; dishes like crème brûlée french toast, pastrami on rye Benedict, and quinoa porridge are great alternatives to standard breakfast/brunch fare and have inspired many a breakfast table dispute over who gets the last bite.

Heirloom Fine American Cookery, Chestnut Hill; 8705 Germantown Ave., Philadelphia, PA 19118; (215) 242-2700; heirloomdining.com; New American; $$$. Veteran Philadelphia Chef Al Paris brings upscale comfort food to the quaint neighborhood of Chestnut Hill with his new eatery. At the 50-seat BYOB, the menu reveals a thoughtful focus on seasonal, local produce and true American ingredients as evidenced in dishes like a lightly dressed beet and walnut salad paired with a chèvre croquette and meltingly tender smoked pulled chicken atop an airy biscuit in a delightful cumin-scented broth. A self-proclaimed cookbook antiquarian, Paris's love of vintage recipes and cooking techniques manifests itself as an edited menu of reconfigured American classics that borrow from the South, New England, and even the Midwest. Heirloom's dinner menu offers a trek across the country—shrimp and scallop purloo with tasso ham and gold rice is a nod to South Carolina's Low Country while the lamb porterhouse with red chile–spiked glaze celebrates the big, bold flavors of the West. Sunday brunch presents the same focus on seasonal ingredients with a menu of familiar staples with Paris's signature twists. Traditional eggs Benedict get an appetizing makeover with crab cakes and a piquant Hollandaise and humble brussels sprouts are simply sautéed with diced bacon and grapes and elevated to something pretty special. See Chef Paris's recipe for **Heirloom Spoonbread** on p. 245.

Honey's Sit 'n Eat, Northern Liberties; 800 N. 4th St., Philadelphia, PA 19123; (215) 925-1150; honeys-restaurant.com; Southern/Soul; $$. You'll be hard-pressed to find a more hybrid menu than the one at Honey's. A mash-up of traditional American soul food and Jewish standards, Honey's Sit 'n Eat is the Northern Liberties answer to South Philly's popular **Sabrina's Cafe** (p. 50). Nestled on the corner of a neighborhood side street, the kitschy warehouse-turned-restaurant gets a lot of foot traffic from those seeking the signature latkes, homemade jams, and local Lancaster produce. With dishes like *enfrijoladas* (flour tortillas filled with scrambled eggs and beans, topped with salsa verde, black bean puree, and *queso fresco*), open-faced biscuit sandwiches, and bagels and lox, the extensive menu is as funky and eclectic as the decor. Cash only.

Koo Zee Doo, Northern Liberties; 614 N. 2nd St., Philadelphia, PA 19123; (215) 923-8080; koozeedoo.com; Portuguese; $$$. The name of the restaurant is a phonetic play on the Portuguese word *cozido,* meaning "cooked," and dishing up simply prepared food in an effort to preserve their distinctive and unique flavors is where this

Northern Liberties eatery shines. Cozy and comforting, Koo Zee Doo offers a variety of authentic plates that pay tribute to owner Carla Gonaçalves's Portuguese roots by utilizing the full spectrum of meat—sometimes the whole animal. From *arroz de pato* (baked duck rice) to *moelas* (braised chicken gizzards), meat is prepared in a variety of ways and usually paired with a simple salad, rice, or potatoes. Specials are run daily, but Thursday night is an especially delightful treat with roasted suckling pig topping the menu. Closed Tues.

Kurth's Seafood, North Philadelphia; 901 W. Susquehanna Ave., Philadelphia, PA 19122; Seafood; $. Completely unpretentious and located in the oft-overlooked heart of North Philly, take-out-only Kurth's has been a neighborhood staple for over 70 years. A restaurant isn't graced with that kind of longevity without serving some seriously good eats and Kurth's is no exception. The menu is not necessarily geared to the health-conscious as most of the offerings are deep-fried, but indulging in cracker-crusted fried fish, hand-cut fries, and a side of coleslaw is an occasional indulgence to be savored calorie by calorie.

Llama Tooth, North Philadelphia; 1033 Spring Garden St., Philadelphia, PA 19123; (267) 639-4582; llamatooth .com; New American; $$. The old adage warns not to judge a book by its cover, but you should definitely judge this restaurant by its title. The name alone just oozes an eclectic, funky, cool vibe and the newly opened restaurant doesn't disappoint. The walls are

Sugar High

Philadelphia has a rich confectionery history and a number of those landmark chocolatiers and artisanal sweets purveyors still exist today. From retro ice cream shops to the revival of lost candy artistry, the city takes its love of sugar seriously. The sheer number of bakeries, confectioneries, chocolatiers, and ice cream shops confirm what most already know: Sometimes only a sugary, ooey gooey, sprinkle-studded, frosting-topped treat will do.

Famous 4th St. Cookie Company, *Market East; 51 N. 12th St., Philadelphia, PA 19107; (215) 629-5990; famouscookies.com; Cookie Shop.* There aren't many things in life that are better than a hot, gooey chocolate chip cookie straight from the oven. Butter-rich and hefty, this Reading Terminal Market cookie shop may be a nightmare for your diet but there's never been a more worthy saboteur. There's an almost endless supply of oatmeal raisin, Snickerdoodle, and macadamia nut–studded chocolate chip wonders and, though a bit pricey, it's a nice way to reward yourself.

The Franklin Fountain, *Old City; 116 Market St., Philadelphia, PA 19106; (215) 627-1899; franklinfountain.com; Ice Cream Shop.* Eric and Ryan Berley, theatrical candy makers and time travelers, are at it again with their Shane Confectionery (below) counterpart. Paper hat–bedecked soda jerks, honest-to-goodness egg creams and thick, creamy homemade ice cream are what you'll find at this old timey ice cream shop. With an antique storefront and authentic period accoutrements gracing the inside (including an old-fashioned cash register), you may forget what era it is—especially with cutely worded wall signs reminding customers of the cash-only policy. Gargantuan treats like the Mt. Vesuvius (an ice cream sundae with brownies, homemade hot fudge, and a healthy smattering of malt powder and whipped cream) and the Stock Market Crunch (rocky road ice cream doused with peanut butter sauce and topped with a crumbling of salt pretzels) may require the help of a partner or two in order to sufficiently tackle the dessert.

Marcie Blaine Artisanal Chocolates, *Midtown Village; 108 S. 13th St., Philadelphia, PA 19107; (215) 546-8700; marcieblaine.com; Chocolatier.* Marcie Turney and Valerie Safran, the reigning doyennes of Midtown Village, count this artisanal chocolate shop among their growing 13th Street empire (see **Barbuzzo,** p. 73 and **Lolita,** p. 81). When taking a break from butchery at one of their restaurants, Turney works her magic in her eponymous sweets boutique, crafting beautiful, uniquely flavored chocolate candies. Ingredients like organic cream and butter are sourced from nearby Lancaster County while seasonal produce, honey, and herbs are gathered from local farms. The result is a concise menu of small-batch flavors like Champagne-infused dark chocolate ganache, grape balsamic, and banana tahini.

Shane Confectionery, *Old City; 110 Market St., Philadelphia, PA 19106; (215) 922-1048; shanecandies.com; Chocolatier/Confectionery.* Sporting muttonchops and outfitted in period attire, brothers Ryan and Eric Berley step back in time in their recently refurbished Victorian-era confectionery, doling out small-batch chocolates, rock candy, nut clusters, and their signature buttercreams. Continuing the aesthetic of their nearby retro ice cream shop, **The Franklin Fountain** (above), the fellows here are sticklers for authenticity—large, candy-filled glass jars display their wares while brass scales are used to weigh purchases, conjuring up penny candy nostalgia of a bygone era. Artisanal, fair-trade chocolate can be found in the shop, but most of the candy is made upstairs using fresh ingredients. Just as with the theatrics and costumes, the Berleys fully commit to the artistry of candy-making by turning out what are, arguably, some of the best candies around.

splattered with bright, vibrant colors and, although the interior is a bit sparse and dated, the outside dining is the real attraction. A bamboo gate, jauntily draped strings of lights and wall murals make this place a definite date-night destination. New American takes on dishes like creamy crab mac and cheese, eggplant fries, and a succulent lamb burger are menu standouts while cheekily named drinks like the Pain Killer and Llamarita (a margarita made with orange juice and nutmeg) are sure to please the adventurous.

Makiman Sushi, Far Northeast; 7324 Oxford Ave., Philadelphia, PA 19111; (215) 722-8800; Japanese; $$. There's no getting around it—Northeast Philadelphia is a tough, hardscrabble town and its dining scene hasn't gotten much attention especially since many suburbanites wouldn't imagine venturing to its inner folds for a bite to eat. This scrappy corner of Philly is overflowing with greasy takeout spots and fast-food joints, so finding a diamond in the rough like Makiman Sushi is indeed a rarity. Those with a sense of humor and a penchant for whimsy will like oddly named sushi rolls like Northeast Viking, Sixers, and Captain Crunch (it remains a mystery whether or not the eponymous cereal is an actual ingredient). Diners whose feet are steadfastly planted in tradition will appreciate the spicy tuna rolls and dumpling soup.

McCrossen's Tavern, Fairmount; 529 N. 20th St., Philadelphia, PA 19130; (215) 854-0923; mccrossens.com; Traditional American; $$. At first glance, McCrossen's appears to be a typical neighborhood bar catering to the blue-collar regulars, but further inspection of this unassuming North Philadelphia taproom finds pretty impressive beer and wine lists and not only a customary but well-prepared menu of pub favorites but also some welcome surprises. While Philly bar owners seem uncomfortable carrying the mantle of being called gastropubs, elevating diners' notions of bar food by serving veal sweetbreads, braised Berkshire pork belly with a white-bean cassoulet, or marinated *boquerones* (white anchovies) is a surefire (and tasty) way to earn the title. For the thirsty, Sunday brunch is an amazing offer—$20 will get you an entree and unlimited Bloody Marys or mimosas. Patrons fearful that their everyman bar is morphing into a pretentious hipster hangout needn't worry—McCrossen's still does a fine job of burgers, wings, and sandwiches and continues to live up to its reputation as being the place to grab an after-work beer.

Memphis Market & Grill, Kensington; 2327 E. Huntington St., Philadelphia, PA 19125; (215) 426-1917; Traditional American/Sandwiches; $. If you don't live in the immediate area, chances are you have never heard of this place and that's a pity. One can't call himself a true foodie until crossing the threshold of a place like this. The tiny neighborhood corner store is a no-frills spot that just happens to churn out great breakfast and lunch options. A pork roll and cheese sandwich, a side of breakfast potatoes, and a coffee will only set you back about $8, and the hoagies compete with those from better-known places; the shelves are stocked with the usual corner-store wares.

Mica, Chestnut Hill; 8609 Germantown Ave., Philadelphia, PA 19118; (267) 335-3912; micarestaurant.com; New American; $$$$. Since its critically acclaimed opening, Mica has set the blogosphere and the suburban dining scene ablaze and has been declared a neighborhood gem. *Food & Wine* recently included Mica's artichoke agnolotti on its coveted "Top 10 Restaurant Dishes" list. It's been a fantastical ride for Chef-Owner Chip Roman, whose additional eateries, Ela and **Blackfish** (p. 209) have garnered similar praise. The menu is seasonally focused and dishes are crafted from the freshest ingredients available as evidenced in the rotating menu. Choice selections include the Barnegat scallops, Cape May skate wing, *carnaroli* risotto, Loch Duart Scottish salmon and *magret* duck breast. A Wednesday night prix fixe tasting menu is an excellent option for those who want to sample the best of the chef's caprices; weekend brunch is impressive as well.

Modo Mio, Northern Liberties; 161 W. Girard Ave., Philadelphia, PA 19123; (215) 203-8707; modomiorestaurant.com; Italian; $$$. Modo Mio is arguably the best casual Italian eatery in Philadelphia and the nightly crowd stands as testament to that fact. Most serious foodies, unwilling to relinquish control over their dining choices, are turned off by prix fixe menus but Modo Mio's *turista* menu—a 4-course feast of rustic Italian fare— is delicious and a steal at $34. This place is Italian food at its finest; those who are looking for Americanized plates of spaghetti

and meatballs should dine elsewhere. Worthy of consideration are the rabbit ravioli and tender veal cheek as is the boar *ragù* and pillowy gnocchi whose delectability make you feel as if you're dining under the Tuscan sun. The restaurant also offers a number of gluten-free options; simply inform the server.

Nifty Fifty's, Far Northeast; 2491 Grant Ave., Philadelphia, PA 19195; (215) 676-1950; niftyfiftys.com; Traditional American; $. With "oldies but goodies" blaring through the speakers, you half expect to see girls in bobby socks and poodle skirts when you step into this kitschy time machine; the nostalgia is almost palpable. Naysayers and food snobs may dismiss this place because it's a local chain (there are three Pennsylvania locations), but the menu is simple but fresh and done well; classics like cheesesteaks, burgers, hot dogs (the bacon-wrapped Cheez Whiz–doused Texas Tommy is a crowd-pleaser) and cheese fries (hailed as quite possibly the best in the city) are served alongside a seemingly endless bevy of thick, rich milk shakes. Children and the chemistry-minded alike enjoy concocting customizable sodas limited only to one's imagination.

North Third, Northern Liberties; 801 N. 3rd St., Philadelphia, PA 19123; (215) 413-3666; norththird.com; New American; $$. With a winning trifecta of attentive service, an outstanding menu and a relaxed vibe, restaurant/bar North Third has earned a special place in the hearts of diners and drinkers alike. Elevated bar food like peanut-studded Asian-style chicken wings and steamed mussels in a Thai coconut curry sauce are delicious and punched-up just enough to remind you that you're not dining at a dive bar or greasy spoon. For liquid seekers, there is a dizzying array of cocktails and beers on tap as well as a decent wine list—if you leave here thirsty, it's your own fault.

Osteria, Fairmount/Avenue of the Arts North; 640 N. Broad St., Philadelphia, PA 19130; (215) 763-0920; osteriaphilly.com; Italian; $$$. When famed Chef-Restaurateur Marc Vetri opened his casual Italian eatery on North Broad, critics thought he was insane. After all, the street has earned the dubious honor of being one of the sketchiest in the city and not exactly the place you'd expect a James Beard Award–winning chef to set up shop, but Vetri's insanity paid off. The spacious, industrial dining room is a diner's dream—offering views of the open kitchen and a wood-burning brick oven. For the true gourmand and serious food historian, eye candy in the form of a vintage Faema coffee machine and Berkel prosciutto slicer are enough to make one swoon. More casual than that of its Center City sibling **Vetri** (p. 98), the menu offers up rustic dishes like chicken liver rigatoni and simply prepared wood-grilled octopus with cured lemon. A variety of thin-crust brick oven pizzas like the Parma (mozzarella, fontina, arugula, and prosciutto di Parma) are true standouts and not to be missed.

Paesano's, Northern Liberties; 152 W. Girard Ave., Philadelphia, PA 19123 (additional location in the Italian Market); (267) 886-9556; paesanosphillystyle.com; Italian/Sandwiches; $. It's hard to imagine that a guy with a decidedly un-Italian surname would be the force behind some of the best Italian food in the city, but it's true (see **Monsu**, p. 138 and **Modo Mio**, p. 44). Chef-Owner Peter McAndrews has proven that you don't necessarily have to be a *paesan* to know your way around a *cucina*. His tiny, unassuming shop pays homage to the humble sandwich in a way that no other place in the city does. Fair warning: one look at the chalkboard menu and all of your decision-making abilities will be rendered useless—it's simply too hard to suppress your inner glutton and choose just one sandwich. The Arista with roasted suckling pig, Italian long hots, broccoli rabe, and sharp provolone, or the Gustaio with house-made lamb sausage, sun-dried cherry *mostarda,* Gorgonzola spread, roasted fennel, and arugula? Why choose just one? A menu on which nothing is over $10 practically begs you to walk out with a bag full of the best sandwiches in the city.

PYT, Northern Liberties; 1050 N. Hancock St., Philadelphia, PA 19123; (215) 964-9009; pytphilly.com; Traditional American/ Burgers; $$. First things first, this is not your mama's burger joint—that is, unless she's a skinny jean–wearing hipster with an affinity for crazy-loud music. This is definitely the place where the cool kids go. PYT (which stands for "Pay Yer Tab") is a fun hangout where you can grab a burger and beer and people-watch to your heart's content which—if weather permits—is better if you take advantage of the outdoor seating on the open-air piazza. If blaring music and the occasional video game tournament is not your scene, you may want to consider dining elsewhere, but that would mean missing out on favorites like the cheesesteak pretzel roll burger and the pistachio-crusted lamb burger. Traditionalists may opt for the eponymous PYT burger which is simply a cheeseburger, but creative types who want to spiff up their burgers would be smart to order the PYT and pile on additional toppings like avocado, fried egg, and the "special" sauce. A side of the Kenzinger-battered onion rings is an absolute necessity as is an "adult milk shake" where booze and ice cream come together in a rather tasty combination. While a little pricey at $10, they are way more fun to down than the nonalcoholic sort.

Rib Rack, Oxford Circle; 2100 Tyson Ave., Philadelphia, PA 19149; (215) 338-9399; Barbecue; $$. Smoky, fall-off-the-bone meats, some honest-to-goodness sides, and conceivably the best corn muffins around are what keep diners coming back to this off-the-beaten-path barbecue joint. Wings, gargantuan sandwiches, and burgers are thrown in for good measure and the

stuffing and gravy, while not normally considered a typical pairing to barbecue, are definitely worth a try. While it's a little too dimly lit, dining here is like joining a secret society; it feels as if only the initiated know the location of this tucked away neighborhood eatery but once you find it, it will surely become part of your regular rotation.

Ristorante Longano, Far Northeast; 9363 Old Bustleton Ave., Philadelphia, PA 19115; (215) 698-0700; cafelongano.com; Italian; $$. Neighborhood residents are very protective of this once-hidden gem, but the secret is out—Ristorante Longano (formerly Cafe Longano) is one of the best BYOBs in Northeast Philadelphia. Having undergone major renovations recently, the restaurant shed its former casual brick oven pizza image and traded it for a more grown-up one and a menu focused on the use of fresh ingredients and handmade pastas. Fettuccine that is made in-house in the morning finds itself tossed in a light tomato sauce with peppers; house specialty Chicken Longano is simply but beautifully prepared saltimbocca-style with a mild wine sauce. Other mainstays include chicken marsala and tiramisu for dessert, but don't discount these classics—it's Italian cooking at its finest.

Rustica, Northern Liberties; 903 N. 2nd St., Philadelphia, PA 19123; (215) 627-1393; rusticaphilly.com; Italian/Pizzeria; $. Seating is limited and cramped in this NoLibs (Northern Liberties) spot, but well worth the elbow or two you may have to take (or give) to jockey for position in line. As its name implies, the food here is prepared deftly and simply; nothing is overwrought. Pizzas come in the red and white varieties and are crafted from fresh ingredients. With sandwiches like the Tartufo, Rustica waves a magic wand over the humble cheesesteak and transforms it into something other-worldly with a smattering of truffle cream and caramelized onions; wings, salads, and calzones round out the menu. If weather permits, it may be wise to snag a seat outside to enjoy your slice in peace.

Sabrina's Cafe & Spencer's Too, North Philadelphia; 1804 Callowhill St., Philadelphia, PA 19130; (215) 636-9061; sabrinas cafe.com; Traditional American; $$. Seriously, Philadelphia should change its motto to the "City of Bruncherly Love"; this is a town that places brunch on (almost) equal footing with the cheesesteak. In other words, brunch is pretty important and Sabrina's does it well. Dessert is disguised as breakfast in the form of stuffed french toast with a heaping mound of cream cheese/mascarpone filling, chocolate chips, fresh berries, and infused syrup and, while it may very well put you in a calorie-induced coma, it's well worth it. Breakfast staples like eggs Benedict and huevos rancheros are divine. In case you're not an early riser, Sabrina's does a respectable job of dinner as well—a juicy Angus burger rests atop a sour cream–chive biscuit and is adorned with cheddar, caramelized onions, maple shallot-onion jam, and an over-easy egg.

Sazon Restaurant & Cafe, Spring Garden; 941 Spring Garden St., Philadelphia, PA 19123; (215) 763-2500; sazonrestaurant.com; Latin American; $$. Often overlooked, Sazon is one of those hidden neighborhood gems that flies under the radar because of location. But the fact that only street parking is offered and it's cash only shouldn't be a deterrent, or else you will miss some pretty amazing Venezuelan cuisine. The *sancocho de carne* (exotic beef stew) with homemade hot sauce is spicy and hearty; the arepas (unleavened patty of cornmeal or flour) provide the perfect vehicle for an interesting Latin American sandwich. To cap off the meal, you can't go wrong with sugary homemade churros and velvety chocolate dipping sauce.

Sid Booker's, Logan; 4600 N. Broad St., Philadelphia, PA 19140; (215) 329-4455; Seafood; $. Even though this North Philadelphia shrimp shack sits squarely at the mouth of a heavily trafficked interchange and is brightly lit by the huge sign that hovers above the tiny cash-only takeout, daring to venture to this part of town often is usually not an option for the faint-hearted—and it really should be. Sure, thick bulletproof glass separates patrons from the servers and service tends to get brisker as the line gets longer, but the fried shrimp from Sid's rivals those from the finest establishments. There's no pretention here—fried shrimp seasoned with a bit of salt and pepper and a dash of hot sauce and a choice of three sides are all that grace this uncomplicated menu. Like many takeout joints dotted around the city, there are ordering rules: Don't order fries (or any side dish) if you're not ordering shrimp or be prepared to be given the cold shoulder. Don't forget to bring a drink if you plan on delving into your shrimp on the way home as there are no drinks served here.

Silk City Diner & Lounge, Northern Liberties; 435 Spring Garden St., Philadelphia, PA 19123; (215) 592-8838; silkcityphilly.com; New American; $$. Silk City is one of those rare successful restaurant/nightclub anomalies that manage to provide outstanding food and a vibrant night scene. Chowing down on Thai chili-glazed wings while swaying to the beat of the in-house DJ is highly encouraged and so is, weather permitting, getting your drink (and grub) on outside in the beer garden. Open until the wee hours of the morning, the all-encompassing menu also accommodates those who are in the throes of a hangover with tasty breakfast offerings like Belgian waffles and smothered chicken and waffles. Now, that's a party.

Sketch, Fishtown; 413 E. Girard Ave., Philadelphia, PA 19125; (215) 634-3466; sketch-burger.com; Traditional American/Burgers; $$. The good folks at Sketch are helpful enough to provide an anatomy of their popular burgers on their website, showing you how to craft the perfect burger and they would know. A burger is not just a burger here—it's an experience. Sandwiched between buns from famed area restaurant/bakery **LeBus** (p. 27), the burgers are anything but average. Ordering the smashed onion or truffle butter burger off the menu is a sure thing, but crafting your own to suit your whimsy is more fun. Just be sure not to ask for ketchup—unless you want to get a (friendly) tongue-lashing from the staff. A better choice would be the spicy harissa aioli or one of the many homemade sauces available; a lace-edged fried egg adds a little something extra. Thick milk shakes and hand-cut fries are a sure thing.

Sonata, Northern Liberties; 1030 N. American St., Philadelphia, PA 19123; (215) 238-1240; sonatarestaurant.com; New American; $$. The menu at Sonata—no pun intended—plays a sweet song indeed. The butter-poached lobster pot pie is a deconstructed version of the classic with a light, almost millefeuille-like biscuit perched atop the tasty mélange. Diners who have eschewed their carnivorous ways will enjoy vegetarian plates like the zucchini and *halumi* fritter with tomato confit and eggplant puree. The pared-down menu handsomely rewards the taste buds with sophisticated, thoughtfully executed fare.

Steve's Prince of Steaks, Far Northeast; 7200 Bustleton Ave., Philadelphia, PA 19149; (215) 338-0985; stevesprinceofsteaks.com; Traditional American; $. Steve may humbly refer to himself as a prince, but to many he's a king. The Northeast battle for sandwich supremacy between Steve's and rival Jim's is as intense as the age-old South Philly cheesesteak war that has been brewing between Geno's and Pat's for decades. Steve's is a prototypical corner sandwich shop that has mastered the art of constructing a proper cheesesteak, which a true Philadelphian will tell you consists of the holy trinity of bread, cheese, and meat. While Steve's does offer additional toppings, you'll be sniffed out as a tourist if you order anything other than fried onions to adorn your cheesesteak. Cash only (ATM is located inside).

Sweet Lucy's Smokehouse, Far Northeast; 7500 State Rd., Philadelphia, PA 19136; (215) 333-9663; sweetlucys.com; Barbecue; $$. If there is such a thing as meat eaters' heaven, this place is it. Ribs, brisket, chicken, kielbasa, and even turkey get bathed in woodsy smoke and lightly swathed in sauce. In a barbecue joint, side dishes usually play second fiddle to the meat but not at Sweet Lucy's. Don't be surprised if you find yourself standing in line a second (or third) time to score additional squares of cornbread or a bowl of mac and cheese.

Tacconelli's Pizzeria, Port Richmond; 2604 E. Somerset St., Philadelphia, PA 19134; (215) 425-4983; tacconellispizzeria.com; Pizza; $$. First things first, snagging a pie at Tacconelli's is an experience that involves calling ahead to reserve your pizza dough and enduring crowds and guaranteed long wait times while the pizza cooks. Side note: Since it's a BYOB, the experience can be made tolerable by bringing along copious amounts of alcohol—on any given day, Tacconelli's could easily be mistaken for a parking-lot tailgate on game day. Regarded by many as the best pizza in the city, there are a limited number of pies made daily so calling ahead (a day or two in advance for large parties, about an hour for everyone else) is mandatory. The thin cracker crust pizza is generously sauced and topped with a sparse sprinkling of cheese and arrives perfectly charred and blistered from the famed brick oven. While there are a number of toppings available, highlights include the margherita, white, and regular varieties.

Taco Riendo, Northern Liberties; 1301 N. 5th St., Philadelphia, PA 19122; (215) 235-2294; Mexican; $$. Condolences to those whose tacos come with a tagline or are marketed by a talking chihuahua. Authentic Mexican cuisine is within your grasp in the trendy neighborhood of Northern Liberties. Many a taqueria is judged by its *al pastor* and Taco Riendo not only passes the test but even throws the palate for a pleasant loop with bits of fresh pineapple in this juicy, brightly flavored spicy delight. Legions of residents flock here daily to grab foil-wrapped burritos and nosh on over a dozen variations of tacos. When you cross the threshold and hear the snippets of Spanish being spoken amid the background music and smell the authentic cooking wafting from the kitchen, it's hard to believe you're not on an island or in a Mexican villa. Sample some *sopes de chorizo* and *tortas* washed down with a glass of real-deal *horchata* and it's hard to believe you're in Philly. Cash only.

Tierra Colombiana, Hunting Park; 4535 N. 5th St., Philadelphia, PA 19140; (215) 324-6086; tierrarestaurante.com; Latin American; $$. To dine at Tierra Colombiana is to take a wild ride through a number of Latin cuisines—Cuban, Dominican, and Colombian dishes are served alongside one another on the extensive menu. Start off with a complimentary basket of buttery, garlicky grilled Cuban bread then delve into authentic platters of arroz con pollo or perfectly seasoned *ropa vieja* that are, for the generous, large enough to share but be advised that your inner glutton will want to hoard every forkful for yourself. For those seeking variety, the *picada* is a mixed plate of sweet and fried green plantains, cassava, steak, fried pork, Colombian sausage, and a few other hand-selected delights. In your search for adventure and authenticity, don't overlook the seemingly standard salsa—you'd be hard-pressed to find better in the city. After feasting, head next door to the restaurant's nightclub and dance off the calories.

Tiffin, Northern Liberties; 710 W. Girard Ave., Philadelphia, PA 19123; (215) 922-1297; tiffin.com; Indian; $$. Indian phenom Tiffin is a chain restaurant with several locations dotted in and around the city, but don't let the stigma of it being a chain discourage you from sampling classics like *malai kofta* or *saag paneer*. Indian cuisine is slowly emerging from behind the curtain that had once kept it largely shadowed, but even timid diners will find Tiffin's menu approachable with a variety of tikka and masalas. The cuisine accommodates both vegetarians and meat-eaters alike.

Trio, Francisville/Fairmont; 2624 Brown St., Philadelphia, PA 19130; (215) 232-8746; triobyob.com; Thai; $$. On the menu at this BYOB, delicious Thai classics like pad thai share space with the popular drunken noodles. A curried cauliflower soup is packed with flavor and imparts a bit of spice on the palate but not so much as to be overpowering. Even die-hard carnivores will appreciate the tofu with ginger—a mélange of sautéed vegetables and triangles of crispy tofu. The deep-fried beggar's pouches filled with crab and shrimp come with a tangy but sweet chile sauce. As is customary at most Thai restaurants, a dish's spiciness can be adjusted using a 1 to 5 rating. Surprisingly (and oddly), an array of American desserts are served— with the pumpkin cheesecake rating high on everyone's must-try list.

Ugly Moose, Roxborough/Manayunk; 443 Shurs Ln., Philadelphia, PA 19128; (215) 482-2739; theuglymoose.com; New American; $$. The unpretentious, laid-back vibe of this Manayunk spot make it one of the coolest watering holes in the area. Ski lodge–like in its decor with a staff as attentive and friendly as winter ski instructors, traditional American fare like steaks and crab cakes are done simply but deliciously. You simply can't have dinner at a place called Ugly Moose without trying the Fat Daddy's Prison Shank Meatloaf—a veal, beef, and pork winner served with creamy mashed Yukon Gold potatoes. Beer lovers will drool over the wide-ranging offering of pale ales and microbrews on the rotating draft list.

Uzbekistan, Far Northeast; 11901 Bustleton Ave., Philadelphia, PA 19116; (215) 671-1990; Russian; $$. Russian and Uzbek cuisines are still largely unfamiliar to most, but the menu at this northern Philadelphia eatery serves a wonderful primer. Large meat-, spice-, and vegetable-filled dumplings called *manti* are a delicious and filling way to delve into the mysteries of the eastern hemisphere. A hearty tomato-based red sauce accompanies a *cherubek*—a large, crescent-shaped pastry filled with a flavorful meat mixture that is usually sold in Russian street food kiosks; seasoned, grilled meat is offered kebab-style and served with the same red sauce. Portions are large, filling, and served family-style, making sharing ideal.

Post-Midnight Munching

The Dapper Dog, Northern Liberties; 2nd & Poplar Streets, Philadelphia, PA 19123; (203) 887-8813; thedapperdog.org; Hot Dogs/Late Night; $. Dapper indeed. Here, hot dogs get dressed

up with some of the quirkiest toppings known to man. The insomniacs who own and operate this late-night mobile food cart will slap just about anything you can imagine on your dog—asparagus, fried egg, peppers, and potatoes. Offerings range from tame—like a traditional Coney Island hot dog—to odd (but delicious) like the "Moe Green" which is an asparagus-topped hot dog with sharp provolone and parmesan. After 2 a.m., you can request any combination of their remaining food be made into a sandwich—yes, the pair has fulfilled requests for pepperoni and mac & cheese sandwiches. The cart's home base is an outdoor patio space in Northern Liberties but check the website for location and menu updates.

Johnny Brenda's, Fishtown; 1201 Frankford Ave., Philadelphia, PA 19125; (215) 739-9684; johnnybrendas.com; Gastropub/Music Venue/Late Night; $$. Having shaken off its former bad vibes as a sketchy neighborhood tavern, Johnny Brenda's reemerged and reinvented itself and is now one of the best bars and music venues in the area—and their menu is nothing to sneeze at, either. Homemade baba ghanoush and hummus and grilled octopus are unexpected but pleasing late night snacks and are as satisfying as a burger and fries, which also make an appearance on the menu. There's a full range of liquor and wine served, but most drinkers head here to see what's on tap—and there are plenty of taps, too—10 to be exact, and 2 hand pumps, which allow for the serving of cask ale. JB's further endears itself to the neighborhood crowd by offering a selection of beers from local breweries.

Machismo Burrito Bar, Roxborough/Manayunk; 4330 Main St., Philadelphia, PA 19127; (215) 508-3333; machismoburritobar .com; Mexican/Late Night; $. No one's ever set out after midnight looking for pretentious, pricey food. Chances are, your late-night cravings are of the cheap, fast "rolled-up-in-a-tortilla" variety. A huge, overstuffed carnitas burrito kicked up a notch thanks to a few shakes from one of the several hot sauces available is just the thing to answer hunger's call. If making snap decisions in rapid succession is not one of your strengths, you may need to sit it out—Machismo's employs the "have-it-your-way" ordering method in which you choose from a variety of meats, fillings, and tortilla flavors. Bonus points for the saffron rice and the more-than-decent vegetarian offerings.

North Bowl, Northern Liberties; 909 N. 2nd St., Philadelphia, PA 19123; (215) 238-2695; northbowlphilly.com; Traditional American/ Late Night; $$. North Bowl is probably the bowling alley you dream of building in your mega-mansion once you hit the lottery. With 17 bowling lanes, a tricked-out upstairs lounge complete with comfy sofas, an arcade, and pool tables, this Northern Liberties hangout definitely puts the average ten pin alley to shame. Nighttime often finds this place overrun with the über-cool set looking to bowl a few games, and wait times for lanes can run a little long, but you'll realize that hanging out with friends, shooting a game of pool, and noshing on comfort food classics is a pretty awesome consolation prize because, really, what's better than a menu that boasts over 10 different tater tot combinations? Burgers, tacos, sandwiches, and a few vegetarian options round out the menu.

North Third, Northern Liberties; 801 N. 3rd St., Philadelphia, PA 19123; (215) 413-3666; norththird.com; New American/Late Night; $$. A crowded bar can spoil an otherwise pleasant night, but you don't have to worry about jockeying for space at North Third—there's a bar in both the front and back areas. Both are perfect places for sipping a cocktail or having a beer. If liquid's not enough, the menu offers a great selection of starters, sandwiches, and entrees, but be sure to check out the dining room's blackboard for daily specials. Cornmeal crusted then flash-fried, the calamari is top-notch as are the steamed mussels with Thai coconut curry sauce, but it's the pierogies with caramelized onions, sour cream, and chives that diners really seek.

Standard Tap, Northern Liberties; 901 N. 2nd St., Philadelphia, PA 19123; (215) 238-0630; standardtap.com; New American/Late Night; $$. Philadelphia has carried on a love affair with beer since the days of Ben Franklin and, judging by the city's number of taprooms, breweries, and gastropubs, residents still love it. Locally produced craft beers and a rotating menu of styles and seasonals make this multiroom gastropub a beer lover's heaven. While the menu's burgers are tasty, upscale bar food is the norm here—signature dishes include chicken pie, fried smelt, and the popular mussels and sausage. The daily specials, subject to the chef's whims, often include pâtés, terrines, wild game, and whole fish preparations.

Czerw's Kielbasy, Port Richmond/Kensington; 3370 Tilton St., Philadelphia, PA 19134; (215) 423-1707; kielbasyboys.com; Meat Shop; $. Even though there are fruitwood-smoked meats, thick-cut steaks and ground meats available, crossing the threshold of Czerw's (pronounced *shevs*) is like entering sausage Valhalla. Resembling a mechanic's garage more than a kielbasa shop, this hotspot is the place to visit when you don't have a Polish cook at your disposal. Smoked, extra garlic, and Cajun represent just a small sampling of the types of kielbasa offered. Old-fashioned hot dogs, brats, links, and smoked slab bacon would make any meat eater's mouth water, but it's the pierogies that steal the spotlight here. Traditional fillings like potato and sauerkraut are winners, but the newfangled cheesesteak, buffalo chicken, and bacon and cheddar-filled variations are killer and give the old-school 'rogies a run for their money; there are even dessert pierogies. Don't skip picking up some condiments: The fresh barrel sauerkraut, spicy mustard and pickles are spot-on.

Feders Fresh Produce, Fairmount; 1822 Spring Garden St., Philadelphia, PA 19130; (215) 568-8010; federsfresh.com; Grocery/ Produce; $. From the onset, family-owned Feders wins most people over with its fun (and free) sample table that is always overflowing with fresh goodies. After nibbling on free eats, shoppers are then free to continue their love affair while strolling the aisles for fresh, inexpensive produce, cheeses, and homemade pitas, sauces, and hummus. The huge wine selection makes it easy to pick up a bottle of vino to complement your food purchases. Artfully crafted salads and a smoothie/juice bar present healthy options and the warm, friendly staff are happy to offer suggestions and, if you're indecisive, are more than willing to play mad scientist and allow you to taste test various smoothie combinations.

Krakus Market, Port Richmond; 3150 Richmond St., Philadelphia, PA 19134; (215) 426-4336; krakusmarket.com; Meat Shop/Specialty Market; $. The neighborhood of Port Richmond enjoys a large Polish immigrant and Polish-American population and, for foodies, that's a gastronomic blessing. Krakus Market is a market/luncheonette hybrid that offers standards like borscht, potato and cheese pierogies, and kielbasa, but the real treats come in the form of dill meatballs, *golombki* (stuffed cabbage), and fried beets—all of which can be washed down with a $3 Polish beer. If you still have a hankering to satiate your sweet tooth after your kielbasa fest, choose a treat from the extensive dessert menu chock full of authentic sweets. There's also a small selection of Eastern European groceries for those inclined to whip up a Polish feast at home.

The Pink Dolphin, Northern Liberties; 1001 N. 2nd St., Philadelphia, PA 19123; (215) 627-0960; Specialty Grocery/Deli; $.

If you're miffed because your local big-name grocery store doesn't carry Pocky (a type of Japanese candy), Fentiman's old-fashioned sodas, or imported German chocolate bars, you need to mosey down to this Northern Liberties little specialty market—fast. Like most NoLibs shops, the selection here is high-quality, selective, and pricey; but it's completely worth the extra dollar or two to snag hard-to-find goodies that are not readily available elsewhere. Don't forget the little deli area in the back—fresh salads, sandwiches, and panini round out the succinct menu and are perfect for grab-and-go munching. If weather permits, take your snack outside and relax on the piazza where a giant flat-screen TV is mounted on a nearby building's façade.

The Random Tea Room & Curiosity Shop, Northern Liberties; 713 N. 4th St., Philadelphia, PA 19107; (267) 639-2442; therandom tearoom.com; Tea Room; $. Imagine you've been invited for an informal tea to be held in a really cool hippie's living room. Now throw in some oddities, random objects, and a selection of tisanes (herbal or plant infusions used for medicinal purposes) and teas. This is what you get when you visit this cozy tea room. With a variety of loose, hand-blended teas, a knowledgeable and helpful staff, and a totally relaxing environ-ment, this is the ideal place to not only beef up your tea knowledge but also to meditate and clear your mind.

Sorrentino's Grocery, Roxborough/Manayunk; 4361 Cresson St., Philadelphia, PA 19127; (215) 487-0559; Deli; $. It's really easy to walk right past this little tucked-away corner store. Although you'll find a small selection of necessities like milk, eggs, and fresh rolls and buns, Sorrentino's isn't really a grocery store per se. Where this neighborhood gem shines is in its deli section with its host of no-frills but tasty sandwiches. Breakfast sandwiches are great options for commuters and the cheesesteaks here are phenomenal and rival the ones from big-name, better-known establishments. The friendly, everyone-knows-your-name atmosphere makes it the kind of place totally worth searching for.

Center City

Art Museum District, Avenue of the Arts, Chinatown, Logan Square, Market East, Midtown Village, Old City, Penn Center, Queen Village, Rittenhouse Square, Society Hill, South Street District, Washington Square West

When it comes to grabbing the culinary spotlight, Center City siphons most of the attention away from other parts of the city. Over the years, the area has earned a reputation as the best dining spot in Philadelphia and, certainly, the accolades are well deserved. After all, it is home to most of Iron Chef José Garces's Philadelphia restaurant empire and notable options like Barbuzzo, Han Dynasty, Mémé, Vetri, and Zahav. Swank environs, coveted addresses, and an affluent crowd helped skyrocket Center City to culinary rock-star status as evidenced by the sheer number of diners who flood the area on any given night. However, true foodies know that a sky-high price tag is not always synonymous with a great meal and that's what's great about Center City. There is a bevy of inexpensive options dotted around the area—nondescript noodle houses serve steaming bowls of divine pho right around the corner from white tablecloth, haute cuisine establishments—making for an eclectic, interesting and (most importantly) tasty experience.

Landmarks

City Tavern, Old City; 138 S. 2nd St., Philadelphia, PA 19106; (215) 413-1443; citytavern.com; Traditional American; $$$. There are not too many restaurants that offer dishes crafted from the precise recipes of Thomas Jefferson's kitchen staff. Renowned chef Walter Staib, of cookbook and television fame, is considered a master of open-hearth cookery; his menu at City Tavern—an Old City staple since 1773—specializes in 18th-century American fare. Staib replicates colonial standards like mallard duck sausage with sweet and sour cabbage and slow-braised rabbit that would be as comfortable on the table of our forefathers as it is on modern-day tables.

Fountain Restaurant, Logan Square; 1 Logan Sq., Philadelphia, PA 19103; (215) 963-1500; fourseasons.com/Philadelphia; New American; $$$$. Establishments that still enforce a jacket-required decree are fading fast from the dining landscape, but there are a few Philadelphia eateries that cling mightily to the elegance of yesteryear. For decades, the Fountain Restaurant in the Four Seasons

Hotel has been one of the most preferred dining destinations in the city and the recipient of numerous accolades and hospitality awards—including *Forbes Travel Guide*'s 2010 Five-Star award. One look at the elegantly appointed dining room and it becomes apparent why patrons often choose to celebrate their most special moments here. Exquisite views of the bronze cast statues of the Swann Memorial Fountain in the heart of Logan Square are offered from a series of expansive windows and there is, perhaps, nothing more beautiful than the far-reaching views of the majestic architecture of the Benjamin Franklin Parkway at night. Those desiring a more intimate gathering will find the private Logan Room especially accommodating for parties up to 14 guests. While breaths will be taken away by the sheer beauty of Fountain's environs, it is the refined cuisine that garners the most acclaim—including recognition by Zagat as Philadelphia's best restaurant. Diners are presented with the option of ordering a la carte or from the prix fixe menu that rotates at the chef's discretion. Stunning highlights include an offering of fresh seafood and expertly prepared game and beef dishes; olive oil–poached Scottish salmon complemented by a silken Jerusalem artichoke puree and melted leeks surrounded by a moat of Meyer lemon broth is a wonderful indication of Fountain's culinary capabilities. Indulge further by selecting a confection from the decadent dessert menu.

The Floating Restaurant

Boasting a storied chronology, the grand tall ship the *Moshulu* is permanently docked on the Penn's Landing waterfront and is a fine dining attraction that should be added to your culinary bucket list. Private dining rooms and outdoor deck offer sweeping views of the city and the waterfront, but it is the menu that is the true star of this floating landmark. A contemporary American menu peppered with a few ambitious seafood dishes, the *Moshulu* (pronounced *mo-shoe-loo*) has drawn the attention (and praise) of several national outlets and garnered numerous culinary awards. With a flair for whimsy, the menu shows off its adventurous side with the *foie gras* PBJ—seared Hudson Valley *foie gras* atop toasted brioche and scattered with pistachio, cherries, roasted plums, and drizzled with port wine jus. A host of deftly prepared land options are available, but Moshulu shines with its seafood offerings—exactly what you would expect from a nautical restaurant. During warmer months, the multilevel open decks are the ideal place to sip a nighttime cocktail or gather with a group of friends for weekend brunch. For those looking for typical nightclub alternatives, attend one of the fun, DJ-fueled summertime barbecues under the stars against the backdrop of the twinkling light of the Benjamin Franklin Bridge. **Moshulu, Penn's Landing;** *401 S. Columbus Blvd., Philadelphia, PA 19106; (215) 923-2500; moshulu.com; Tradtional American/Seafood; $$$.*

Le Bec-Fin, Rittenhouse Square; 1523 Walnut St., Philadelphia, PA 19102; (215) 567-1000; lebecfin.com; French; $$$$. For decades, the antics of eccentric, sometimes irascible Lyon-born Chef-Proprietor Georges Perrier have garnered as much attention as the food at his Rittenhouse Square landmark. Credited with single-handedly laying the foundation of the Philadelphia haute dining scene, Perrier's menu is pure divinity with a choice of a 4-course, 7-course, or *grande dégustation* 9-course tasting menu of dexter-ously prepared French classics. Indulgent by nature, tender roasted sweetbreads and warm shrimp with burnt-orange vinaigrette and Madeira jus are a delight as is most of the menu. Reaching back into the annals of fine dining, Le Bec-Fin may be the only Philadelphia eatery that still offers a dessert cart—a two-tiered trolley outfitted with the most fanciful and decadent pastries and confections. Known for its white glove service and grandiose dining room, a meal here is not only considered dining but an experience. Recently, Perrier sold the iconic landmark but the new owner (a Thomas Keller alum) promises the same level of commitment to quality but will seek to modernize the menu a bit; for now, the name of the restaurant will remain the same.

Foodie Faves

Alma de Cuba, Rittenhouse Square; 1623 Walnut St., Philadelphia, PA 19103; (215) 988-1799; almadecubarestaurant.com; Latin

American; $$$. Contemporary styling meets old world Latin elegance in this pastel-colored Center City eatery. The über-chic lounge arouses the senses with all the sensuality of a Miami nightclub with traditional Cuban elements woven into the overall landscape; a second-floor balcony-style dining area is as warm and inviting as an *abuela*'s living room. Purists will be pleased to find traditional libations like caipirinhas and mojitos on the cocktail menu as well more innovative creations like the tongue-in-cheek Cohiba—a nod to Cuba's cigar-producing superiority—which includes a dash of house-made cigar bitters. Chef Daniel Rodriguez pays thoughtful homage to his Cuban roots with his "Nuevo Latino" cuisine, infusing traditional dishes with modern flair. Sliders—that ubiquitous appetizer menu staple—get a Cubano makeover with spicy chorizo replacing the usual beef or chicken accompanied by crispy matchstick potatoes, mustard, and pickled slaw. Another dish not to be missed is the *vaca frita*. Literally translated as "fried cow," it is a delightful twice-fried crispy skirt steak seasoned with Cuban oregano and served with rice and beans and a perfectly complementary, lightly-acidic tomato *escabeche*. Alma de Cuba is no slouch on desserts, either—try the award-winning (and local favorite) chocolate cigar—a decadent confection of almond cake rolled in chocolate mousse, dusted with chocolate, and served with *dulce de leche* ice cream.

Amada, Old City, 217-219 Chestnut St., Philadelphia, PA 19106; (215) 625-2450; amadarestaurant.com; Spanish; $$$. Hailed as Philadelphia's first bona-fide tapas restaurant, Amada is the trendy brainchild of Chicago-born José Garces, who claimed the prestigious title of Iron Chef on Food Network's *The Next Iron Chef* series in 2010. Dimly lit and oozing sexiness, the restaurant itself is chicly outfitted with the most comfortable chairs and banquettes imaginable, encouraging the kind of languid dining that allows patrons to luxuriate in the afterglow of a perfect meal. Small plates of authentic cuisine focus entirely on the Andalusian region of Spain with menu highlights including Mediterranean-kissed dishes like *ensalada de jamón,* a mélange of Serrano ham, figs, Cabrales (a Spanish blue cheese) and spiced almonds. The crab-stuffed peppers, or *piquillos rellenos,* and artichoke and wild mushroom  flatbread are perennial favorites, as well as the carefully curated selection of Spanish cheeses. While Amada boasts an impressive wine list, its cocktail menu remains one of the most popular in the city with such enticing, unusual drinks like Law of Desire, Tie Me Up Tie Me Down, and Bad Habits encouraging even the most devout teetotaler to imbibe. Reservations are highly recommended as crowds tend to descend on this popular Center City establishment.

Amis, Washington Square West; 412 S. 13th St., Philadelphia, PA 19147; (215) 732-2647; amisphilly.com; Italian; $$$. In a city full of Italian eateries, it's hard to make a name for oneself, but neighborhood gem Amis has done just that with a sharp, focused menu showcasing clean and simple flavors. Like any good trattoria, Amis takes a few of the freshest high-quality ingredients and elevates them to new heights. Humble pecorino is baked and transformed into something otherworldly with a drizzle of almond honey—the combination of sweet and salty is divine. Pillowy soft gnocchi serve as a perfect foil to a hearty oxtail *ragù* and standards like steamed mussels and arancini get a modern reworking with guanciale and a meat *ragùu* respectively. However, it's "Sal's old-school meatballs" with tomato potato (a strange but tasty concoction not to be questioned) that elicit the most praise—so moist and rich that *nonnas* everywhere should be worried. You'll want to take a deep breath to make room for the *tartufo al bacio,* a chocolate and hazelnut semi-freddo with candied *amarena* cherries.

Audrey Claire, Rittenhouse Square; 276 S. 20th St., Philadelphia, PA 19103; (215) 731-1222; audreyclaire.com; Mediterranean; $$. Restaurateur Audrey Claire Taichman first envisioned her eponymous restaurant as a "neighborhood joint" where guests could come and gather in an intimate, unpretentious setting and nosh on well-executed Mediterranean dishes, and even though it opened nearly 10 years ago, guests still clamor for a seat in the popular BYOB. From spring to early autumn, the large cafe windows remain open, allowing patrons to observe the daily happenings of posh Rittenhouse Square. With a focus on seasonality, the menu changes frequently but dishes like seared brussels sprouts with shaved Parmesan (do yourself a favor and sop up the jus with a thick slice of crusty bread), a varied selection of local cheeses, and grilled octopus with feta remain year-round staples. Daily specials usually include a simply prepared, delicious grilled whole fish. Weekend parties of four or more should book a reservation for after 8:30 pm to avoid being rushed. Cash only.

Barbuzzo, Midtown Village; 110 S. 13th St., Philadelphia, PA 19107; (215) 546-9300; barbuzzo.com; Mediterranean; $$$. This recent Midtown Village newcomer has taken ahold of the city and refuses to let go. With a seriously addictive menu of locally sourced ingredients and a slew of house-made accoutrements, Barbuzzo is like a persistent suitor—it's not going any-where—so it's best to just give in to its sultry advances and prepare yourself for an amazing meal. Imaginative pizzas like the Coniglio, a delightful cacophony of rabbit-hazelnut sausage, San Marzano tomatoes, stinging nettles, olives, and basil, serve as a reminder as to why a seat at Barbuzzo is coveted real estate, while handmade pasta with rich "Sunday supper" pork *ragù* remind you why you booked your reservation three months in advance. The salted caramel *budino,* an Italian egg pudding, has garnered a legion of devoted fans and is one of the most coveted recipes in the city. Silky, creamy, and rich, it inspires the kind of spoon-licking in which one does not usually engage in polite company. If you prefer to do your spoon-licking in private, a to-go six-pack of the famed salted caramel *budino* is available for purchase on the restaurant's website. There is no doubt that a stellar menu and well-executed fare are the highlights of the restaurant, but an impressive cocktail menu with a rotating craft beer selection also makes it a destination for serious liquor devotees and brew lovers alike.

Barclay Prime, Rittenhouse Square; 237 S. 18th St., Philadelphia, PA 19103; (215) 732-7560; starr-restaurant.com; Steak House; $$$$. Famed Philadelphia restaurateur Stephen Starr currently has 19 eateries dotted around the city with Barclay Prime as one of two Philadelphia steak houses in his arsenal (the other being **Butcher and Singer,** p. 75). Even with swank surroundings and a prime location in the former Barclay Hotel (now condominiums), Starr unapologetically engages in a bit of lily-gilding with a decadent menu of the finest offerings. Appetizer sliders, made with Kobe—the Holy Grail of beef—are a standout as well as the prime bone-in rib eye and the indulgent truffle mashed potatoes; mac and cheese also gets the red carpet truffle treatment, making it an absolute must. Sweet scallops get a savory lift from lauded Nueske bacon and prove Barclay Prime has some serious seafood street cred while the playful warm chocolate s'mores dessert confirms that the restaurant doesn't take itself too seriously. If you're feeling super-indulgent, ask for the famed $100 Kobe beef and *foie gras* cheesesteak, which doesn't make an appearance on the menu but can be crafted for those with enough discernment (and cash) to ask.

Butcher and Singer, Rittenhouse Square; 1500 Walnut St., Philadelphia, PA 19102; (215) 732-4444; butcherandsinger.com; Steak House; $$$$. The city of Philadelphia has no shortage of ritzy steak houses but restaurateur Stephen Starr outdoes himself with elegant Butcher and Singer. The dim lights and warm wood tones are an ode to old Hollywood and conjure up images of yesteryear; you fully expect to see the Rat Pack huddled in a corner sharing inside jokes over steaks and cocktails. The menu is classic steak house—steaks, chops, and sea-food—with stunners like the stuffed hash browns showing up to steal the side-dish show. Even the classic dessert standard Baked Alaska makes a charming appearance, proving outstanding food is timeless.

Dim Sum Garden, Chinatown; 59 N. 11th St., Philadelphia, PA 19107; (215) 627-0218; Asian; $. Relegated to a dark corner like a misbehaving child sent to time-out, Dim Sum Garden lives in the perpetual shadow of a towering high-rise hotel, but a superb menu and its "little-engine-that-could" mentality ensure its survival. Dim sum is traditionally served as small, bite-size snacks, but in this small, carry out–style restaurant, the concept remains intact but the portions are much more generous and there is no customary dim sum cart service, either. *Xiao long bao,* pan-fried soup dumplings, are the obvious standouts and come in pork and crab varieties. Those accustomed to eating in fine-dining establishments and are overly concerned with a restaurant's ability to pass a white glove inspection will be turned off, but those in the know will appreciate Dim Sum Garden for what it is—a Chinatown eatery that serves well-spiced, tasty dishes at insanely low prices.

Estia, Rittenhouse Square; 1405 Locust St., Philadelphia, PA 19102; (215) 735-7700; estia restaurant.com; Greek; $$$. At upscale Estia, all the usual Greek suspects make an appearance on the menu—*saganaki,* stuffed grape leaves, and spanikopita to name a few—but are so lovingly crafted that you'd swear someone's *yia-yia* was working magic in the kitchen and, while there's no grandmother slaving over a hot stove, you can taste the freshness and authenticity in every hearty bite. Lamb chops are marinated in a fragrant bath of olive oil, lemon, and a heady bouquet of fresh herbs before being grilled to perfection and fork-tender sea bass is moist and flaky. A notable wine list highlights several labels from Greece.

Fish, Washington Square West; 1234 Locust St., Philadelphia, PA 19107; (215) 545-9600; fishphilly.com; Seafood; $$$. Fish boldly throws its hat into the local, sustainable ring with a succinct menu focused on using fresh, regional seafood and produce—listing the provenance of every dish. Fish's menu changes frequently based on the availability of seafood and gems like the scallops with cauliflower, pine nuts, chorizo, and piquillo peppers are not to be missed. You would be remiss if you didn't try the skate wing in a flavorful puddle of Parmesan broth and melted leeks or the Blue Bay mussels swathed in a Panang curry with lemongrass and smoked coconut.

Garces Trading Company, Washington Square West; 1111 Locust St., Philadelphia, PA 19107; (215) 574-1099 garcestradingcompany .com; New American/Specialty shop; $$$. Once again, Food Network Iron Chef winner José Garces has struck gold with his Center City ode to haute eats. Specializing in European-style bistro fare, artisanal cheeses, and charcuterie and boasting an impressive list of wines, Garces Trading Company is part market, part coffee bar, and restaurant all rolled into one. Quite possibly a food lover's heaven, the swank space houses an olive oil tasting area in addition to serving such dreamy dishes as grilled branzino with tart vinegared tomatoes, a Lyonnaise salad and a sublime potted duck. If you're simply looking to satiate your inner confection gastronome, Garces recently started selling a line of GTC Éclat chocolate bars and an assortment of *macarons* in seasonal flavors like apple, pumpkin, and huckleberry.

Han Dynasty, Old City; 108 Chestnut St., Philadelphia, PA 19106; (215) 922-1888; handynasty.net; Chinese; $$. Owner Han Chiang makes no apologies for separating the men from the boys with his recommendations on spice level—if it's heat you seek, it's heat you get, with levels ranging from 1 (mild) to 10 (mouth-burning). The menu even has a "Kids/Baby Adults" section for the faint of heart who are comfortable with neither spice nor authentic Sichuan cuisine, but beware the public chiding you'll receive if you dare opt for one of the Westernized dishes from this lesser menu. There are a number of highlights on the regular menu including the popular *dan dan* noodles, dry pot-style beef (which arrives in a sizzling mini-wok amidst a fanfare of smoke), and "three cup" chicken. Service is brusque at best, so if a doting, fawning staff is your thing, you will be disappointed. If you are paying with cash, inform your server and receive a 10 percent discount. Call ahead when dining with a large party to score the big round table with the lazy Susan—it makes it far easier to share multiple dishes.

Il Pittore, Rittenhouse Square; 2025 Sansom St., Philadelphia, PA 19103; (215) 391-4900; ilpittore.com; Italian; $$$$. It takes a fair amount of moxie to open an Italian restaurant on a block saturated with a slew of Italian eateries, but Executive Chef and partner Chris Painter has something to prove. After all, his name is on the door—sort of. Pittore is Italian for "painter" and, as his surname suggests, the renowned chef uses the plate as his canvas in this upscale ode to Northern Italian cuisine. Prep your palate with a small starter like the creamy, earthy, and completely addictive mushroom toast then ease your way into heartier fare like the roasted suckling pig with pear *mostarda*. Fresh pappardelle in wild boar *ragù* sounds overwhelming but is surprisingly subtle and exudes all the warmth and taste of authentic comfort food. If you can even fathom dessert, the chocolate *bomboloni* with Nutella filling is the perfect way to end a stellar meal.

Indian Restaurant, Rittenhouse Square; 1634 South St., Philadelphia, PA 19146; (215) 964-9451; indianrestaurantpa.com; Indian; $$. While the folks behind this less-than-creatively-named restaurant may be lacking in the art of nomenclature, they more than make up for it with the food. The solid, moderately priced Indian fare—served in quaint Rittenhouse Square environs—is authentic and a spice aficionado's dream. As is customary in Indian cuisine, there are a large number of vegetarian dishes available, from the aromatic vegetable *korma* to the popular *saag paneer*. While the vegetarian dishes are filling and expertly prepared, meat dishes like the lamb *vindaloo* and chicken *kahari* truly shine. Rose-scented *fimi* or *kulfi* proves to be a sweet culmination to the meal.

Kanella, Washington Square West; 1001 Spruce St., Philadelphia, PA 19107; (215) 922-1773; kanellarestaurant.com; Greek/Cypriot; $$. James Beard Award–nominated Chef-Owner Konstantinos Pitsillides grew up in the coastal town of Limassol, Cyprus, and received a degree in tannery and chemical engineering—initially planning on entering the family business; perhaps that would explain his kitchen wizardry and ability to concoct complex dishes from even the humblest ingredients. Kanella was already on the radar of serious foodies, but an episode of Food Network's *The Best Thing I Ever Ate* catapulted the restaurant to the forefront when singing the praises of the famed "Cyprus breakfast"—a heaping mash-up of olive oil–fried eggs, *halumi*, deliciously salty *lounza* (a type of ham similar to Canadian bacon), and bread.

While brunch is an exciting affair, honestly solid dishes like ground lamb kebabs and *kefalotyri*-crusted veal are enough to make you swoon. Closed Mon.

Khyber Pass Pub, Old City; 56 S. 2nd St., Philadelphia, PA 19106; (215) 238-5888; khyberpasspub.com; Traditional American/Cajun; $$. With a killer music selection and an equally impressive beer list, Khyber Pass Pub entices taste buds with fun, completely indulgent food like Cajun-seasoned bacon grease popcorn and a host of down home–inspired dishes (many of which are vegan and/or vegetarian). From hickory-smoked barbecue platters to New Orleans style muffulettas and po' boys, there are no wrong choices. Don't miss the smoked cheddar fries topped with debris gravy—a tasty gravy made from shredded meat (usually roast beef) and its pan juices.

Lacroix at the Rittenhouse, Rittenhouse Square; 210 W. Rittenhouse Sq., 2nd Fl., Philadelphia, PA 19103; (215) 790-2533; lacroixrestaurant.com; New American/French; $$$$. Serving what the chef calls "progressive international cuisine," Lacroix is for serious gourmands with deep pockets. Located on the second floor of the prestigious Rittenhouse Hotel overlooking the city's chicest town square, Lacroix could easily be dismissed as pretentious and stodgy but to do so would be a travesty. Perfect for both intimate, romantic dining and expense-account business dinners, its quietly elegant and beautifully appointed dining room

is the setting for many a romantic dinner where dishes like seared diver scallops and buttery *foie gras* are deftly prepared. In a city that takes its Sunday brunch quite seriously, Lacroix has mastered the art and has consistently garnered praise for its extensive brunch offerings which even include—gasp—a liquid nitrogen dessert station. Stuffiness be damned, this restaurant gets serious cool points for throwing its hat into the molecular gastronomy ring.

Lazaro's Pizza House, Rittenhouse Square; 1743 South St., Philadelphia, PA 19146; (215) 545-2775; Pizza; $. In a city full of pizzerias, it's hard to distinguish oneself but Lazaro's manages to do so by crafting fresh, tasty pies that have become the pizza of choice for casual pizza eaters and aficionados alike. On an impossibly thin crust, sweet tomato sauce is spirally ladled and topped with fresh veggies and meat. You won't find a wood-fired oven or gourmet toppings (unless you count rounds of fried eggplant as such), but the no-frills, relatively inexpensive pies more than hold their own against fancier counterparts. There is a meager dining space consisting of a few card tables and chairs, which don't exactly exude the warmest ambience, so it's best to snag a slice or whole pie to go. Cash only.

Lolita, Midtown Village; 106 S. 13th St., Philadelphia, PA 19107; (215) 546-7100; lolitabyob.com; Mexican; $$$. Chef Marcie Turney and partner Valerie Safran are credited with revitalizing

The Best of Reading Terminal Market

At 120-year-old **Reading Terminal Market** (51 N. 12th St., Philadelphia, PA 19107; 215-922-2317; readingterminalmarket .org), over 100 vendors gather under one roof to offer fresh produce, meats, seafood, ice cream, fresh-cut flowers, Amish baked goods, and specialty and ethnic foods. As one of the nation's busiest markets, it hosted approximately 6.3 million visitors in 2011—on average, up to 120,000 patrons visit the market every week. It's impossible to experience and sample what the market has to offer in just one visit; from garden-fresh produce to prepared foods to confections, it's easy to see why people keep coming back to this heavily-trafficked market. Be sure to check out these highlights:

Bassetts Ice Cream (215-925-4315): As the nation's oldest ice cream company, family-owned Bassetts has been crafting super-premium ice cream for over 150 years. By far, the most popular flavor is the signature Gadzooks—chocolate ice cream studded with peanut butter brownie pieces, chocolate chunks, and caramel swirl.

Dutch Eating Place (215-22-0425): Sidling up to the counter for breakfast or lunch promises a homey, comforting Pennsylvania Dutch—

once-decrepit 13th Street and transforming it into hipster hangout Midtown Village. The pair own six businesses along the street (five of them are eateries; see **Barbuzzo,** p. 73) and thankfully show no signs of stopping and, for that, residents are grateful because everything these two touch seems to turn to gold and Lolita is no style meal like blueberry pancakes, corned beef hash, or a juicy burger fresh off the griddle. While your waist may not be, a sweet tooth is satisfied by the famous apple dumpling drizzled with heavy cream.

Flying Monkey Bakery (215-928-0340): Treat yourself to a sweet treat from this popular bakery whose decadent *Pumpple,* a mile-high confection with whole apple and pumpkin pies baked into cake layers, consistently sells out; arrive at the market early to score a slice. A host of cupcakes (try the lavender one), whoopie pies, and sugary goodies fill the glass display case and have garnered a huge following.

Sang Kee Peking Duck (215-922-3930): At this outpost of Sang Kee's Chinatown locale, juicy Peking duck and steamed dumplings make for a delicious, affordable meal. Steaming bowls of noodle soup are belly-filling and satisfying.

Tommy DiNic's (215-923-6175): Monstrous, delicious sandwiches are worth tolerating the always-long lines guaranteed to be packed with tourists and hungry lunch-breakers alike. The juicy roast pork sandwich with sharp provolone is a thing of beauty.

exception. In this BYOT (the "T" is for tequila), modern Mexican cuisine skillfully collides with Turney's brilliance to create gorgeous plates like hazelnut-crusted duck breast with sweet plantains and sour cherry salsita served with crunchy matchsticks of jicama slaw. The seemingly unassuming chips and salsa as well as the guacamole are habit-forming—simple fare done in an exceptional manner is the mark of any great restaurant. Do as the menu suggests and bring a bottle of your favorite tequila to pair with the host of creative margarita mixers offered. For those unacquainted with the antiquated and slightly annoying Pennsylvania liquor laws that require beer and wine to be sold separately, there is a state liquor store conveniently located around the corner on 12th and Chestnut; suggested tequilas include: Herradura Añejo, José Cuervo Especial, and Patrón Silver.

Matyson, Rittenhouse Square; 37 S. 19th St., Philadelphia, PA 19103; (215) 564-2925; matyson.com; New American; $$$. This Center City BYOB does casual and sometimes playful food exceptionally well. With an intent focus on "hyper-seasonality," the menu changes frequently depending on the availability of fresh produce and local livestock—from Barnegat Light scallops with truffled celery-root to a simply roasted chicken with sunchokes—nearly every dish is a stunner. Special themed tasting menus are offered weekly and emphasize a different local ingredient. Often shadowed by the celebrity of other well-known restaurants in the area, Matyson sometimes doesn't get the accolades it truly deserves but true foodies know just how special this cozy gem really is. Closed Sun.

Mémé, Rittenhouse Square; 2201 Spruce St., Philadelphia, PA 19103; (215) 735-4900; memerestaurant.com; New American; $$$.

On Sundays, crowds of brunch-goers descend upon Mémé (pronounced *may-may*) for Chef David Katz's wildly popular sweet corn pancakes with *foie gras* and maple butter or the Anson Mills grits topped with shrimp, ham, and a single poached yolk. The *croque madame* is another draw and worth missing a few extra minutes of Sunday morning slumber. Get your fried chicken fix on Thursday with Mémé's famous lunch—don't bother craving anything else; it's the only thing served—with a homemade biscuit, a side, and a beer for $11, it's one of the cheapest (and most delicious) lunches in the city. Dinner is a whimsical walk through Chef Katz's mind with the menu reflecting his ever-changing impulses—consider yourself extremely lucky if you dine on a night when the sizzling mussels or roasted bone marrow are an option. Closed Mon. See Chef David Katz's recipe for **Sizzling Mussels** on p. 248.

Mercato, Midtown Village; 1216 Spruce St., Philadelphia, PA 19107; (215) 985-2962; mercatobyob.com; Italian; $$$. When diners hear the words "cramped," "noisy" and "cash-only," they usually run in the opposite direction, but Chef R. Evan Turney takes every precaution to make sure that doesn't happen, and those precautions come in the form of heaping platefuls of ribbon-like pappardelle with veal, pork, and beef bolognese and shaved Grana Padano and gnocchi with a rich short-rib *ragù*. You get the sense that Mercato means business once you find out there is

not only an impressive cured meat and artisanal cheese list but also a bona-fide olive oil list. With such a commitment to authenticity and quality, imperfections are easily overlooked.

Meritage, Rittenhouse Square; 500 S. 20th St., Philadelphia, PA 19146; (215) 985-1922; meritagephiladelphia.com; Traditional American; $$$. Located a few blocks from the very posh Rittenhouse Square, Meritage is a fine diner's dream. The unpretentious, contemporary seasonal menu is ever changing, which, depending on when you dine, could mean starting out with a summer vegetable tempura or a tender, juicy roasted duck with sweet potato mash and cabbage. Staples like the popular (and delicious) Korean fried chicken exude a kind of comforting charm that keep diners coming back, but exciting bites like the pork and shiitake dumplings or roasted garlic and goat cheese flan with pickled beets and quail egg that occasionally make a menu appearance keep intrigued diners guessing. For dessert, indulge in the pumpkin *pot de crème* or peanut butter bombe with caramelized bananas and currant jelly sauce.

Morimoto, Washington Square West; 723 Chestnut St., Philadelphia, PA 19106; (215) 413-9070; morimotorestaurant.com; Japanese; $$$$. Restaurateur Stephen Starr is widely known for his legion of flashy, over-the-top eateries that seem to crop up with such frequency that diners rarely have time to get used to one before another pops up. Well, diners have certainly gotten used to well-aged Morimoto—Starr's sole sushi oeuvre and one of the oldest restaurants in his stellar lineup. Though the restaurant's name-sake—the renowned Masaharu Morimoto (of *Iron Chef* fame)—is rarely at the helm of the Philadelphia outpost, his absence in no way diminishes the quality of the menu at this Center City gem. Certainly not for the faint of wallet, pricey but artfully arranged rows of sashimi and creative dishes like the lobster *épicé* (8-spiced lobster) are almost too beautiful to consume. Entrees here are complex affairs—the whimsical "Duck Duck Duck" is a technically accomplished masterpiece with its various preparations and textures. For a truly indulgent delight, try the chef's choice *omakase* which offers a primer to the essence of Morimoto's cuisine.

Ms. Tootsie's Soul Food, South Street District; 1312 South St., Philadelphia, PA 19147; (215) 731-9045; kevenparker.net; Traditional American/Southern; $$. Soul food is in desperate need of a good publicist. For years, it has undeservedly gotten a bad reputation for being greasy, sub-par fare but iconoclastic owner KeVen Parker seeks to dispel those unfair notions and restore traditional Southern soul food to its rightful place of glory with a menu of classic and new-school dishes. First off, the coolly slick environs immediately let you know you're in for something different and the smells wafting from the kitchen let you know you're in for something delicious. Ms. Tootsie's is probably most famous for its down-home fried chicken, but it's equally comfortable stepping outside the confines of tradition by crafting winners like honey mustard–lime fried chicken served atop a three-green salad and golden fried spheres of crab mac and cheese. A platter of smothered turkey chops and collard greens flavored with smoked turkey or a generous portion of shrimp and grits will have you imagining you're sitting at your grandma's table, but on second thought, Granny probably didn't have a sky bar, private lounges, and designer chandeliers. See Chef Terrance Clarke's recipe for **Peach Cobbler with Sugar Cookie Crust** on p. 252.

Nan Zhou Hand Drawn Noodle House, Chinatown; 927 Race St., Philadelphia, PA 19107; (215) 923-1550; Chinese; $. A stroll through Chinatown will put you face to face with a number of dining options but very few guarantee dinner and a show. Here, you can watch nimble chefs do their handiwork as they engage in the art of noodle making. The noodles come in two  varieties—drawn and shaved—with the latter being thicker and a tad chewier than their pulled counterparts. The menu is fairly straightforward in its offerings and the heaping bowls of noodles and braised meats are tasty. Like most Asian establishments, Nan Zhou offers diners the opportunity to show off their more adventurous side with a spicy pork ear appetizer which, fear not, isn't at all unlike more familiar cuts of pork.

Percy Street Barbecue, South Street District; 900 South St., Philadelphia, PA 19147; (215) 625-8510; percystreet.com; Barbecue; $$. The owners of **Zahav** (p. 101) struck gold again when they decided to open a barbecue joint on one of the city's busiest streets. It's a tricky endeavor to attempt to nail the authentic flavor of Texas 'cue and with a menu of smokehouse favorites like brisket, baby back ribs, and sausage, they've done the Lone Star State proud—all while keeping in mind the sensibility of Philadelphians and what they really want to eat. Gracing the menu are Southern staples like deviled eggs and fried green tomatoes,  but it's the tangy barbecued turkey tails that have patrons clamoring for tables. If you're dining with a crowd, ordering The Lockhart—a family-style serving of menu favorites—is the way to go. Just be sure to save room for a slice of their killer pecan pie.

Pub & Kitchen, Rittenhouse Square; 1946 Lombard St., Philadelphia, PA 19146; (215) 545-0350; thepubandkitchen.com; New American; $$. At Pub & Kitchen, you're likely to find upbeat servers as well-versed in the beer list as they are in discussing the menu. The restaurant's name might imply that it's simply a lowbrow hangout where you can drink yourself into oblivion while scarfing down forkful after forkful of greasy food, but don't unfairly judge this restaurant by its title. With a menu that changes daily, this is no stereotypically bad pub grub—Pub & Kitchen has a solid reputation for serving simple comfort food made with high-quality ingredients. Borrowing from classic English fare, a platter of crispy fish and chips with mushy peas is a favorite and dry-aged custom-blended burgers made with meat from famed Pat LaFrieda Meats in New York City are definite standouts. P&K also does an outstanding brunch trade; don't miss the beer mimosas. They're a fun and quirky play on standard Champagne mimosas.

Pumpkin BYOB, Rittenhouse Square; 1713 South St., Philadelphia, PA 19146; (215) 545-4448; pumpkinbyob.com; New American; $$$. If the eye-catching bright orange logo doesn't command your attention, the sizable windows, with their promise of a peek into the charming one-room dining area, will. Once inside, an attentive staff serves up delicious green-minded fare like pork loin with quail egg and horseradish. In the spirit of good food that's good for you, Pumpkin's cafe and market showcase local ingredients that are truly local. Owner Hillary Bor's and Chef Ian Moroney's philosophy of supporting neighborhood purveyors by buying area produce, meat, dairy, and cheese means only the freshest food makes it to your plate. If you're a in a rush, be sure to visit the market for

on-the-go eats. For the weekend warriors, every Sunday Head Chef Ian Moroney and Chef de Cuisine Chris Kearse lead a free, interactive walking tour—known as "Shop with the Chefs"—through **Headhouse**

Market (p. 204), the city's premier farmers' market. Space is limited; check the restaurant's website for details and registration. Closed Mon.

The QUICK FIXX, South Street District; 1511 South St., Philadelphia, PA 19146; (267) 273-1066; thequickfixx.com; Italian; $. In the city, it's often slim pickings when you're craving late night eats that don't involve pizza, a burger, or a burrito from the drive-thru. This South Street restaurant's name may imply that it's another fast-food joint, but it's not. While the food here is fast, it's fresh and on par with the quality one would find in fine dining establishments. Proving that late night does not have to be synonymous with sub-par, the menu consists of an array of artisanal grilled flatbreads, homemade pastas, creative salads, and bruschettas. The Smoky Roman—fresh pasta in cream sauce with smoked bacon and cheese—should be enjoyed no matter what time of the day.

R2L, Rittenhouse Square; 50 S. 16th St., Philadelphia, PA 19102; (215) 564-5337; r2lrestaurant.com; New American; $$$. Two Liberty Place is one of the most coveted addresses in Philadelphia and serves as the home to many of the area's professional athletes. Atop the private residences and ensconced in one of the poshest highrises in Rittenhouse Square, Chef Daniel Stern's R2L is housed on the 37th floor and offers some of the most beautiful and expansive views of the city and boasts an attractive menu. The upscale environs and chic dining room may be intimidating to some, but Stern's tongue-in-cheek dishes like beef and caramelized cipollini "cheesesteaks" are whimsical enough to break the ice with shy diners while a simply prepared but elegant roasted rabbit dish with fresh and pickled squash and yellow steuben gravy satisfies serious devotees who have come to appreciate Stern's take on elevated cuisine. An impressive Sunday brunch features standards like eggs Benedict and a few surprising twists like smoked salmon served on a soft pretzel.

Randazzo's Pizzeria, Rittenhouse Square; 1826 South St., Philadelphia, PA 19146; (215) 546-1566; Pizza; $. Situated squarely across the street from its rival **Lazaro's** (p. 81), Randazzo's is the kind of place that is easy to walk past, but to do so would be a mistake. Built on a foundation of super-thin crust, the pies are perfectly sauced with a garlicky tomato base and generous smattering of cheese. Like most pizzerias in the city, Randazzo's also plies its trade in sandwiches, wings and cheesesteaks; eggplant parm, Italian chicken cutlet sandwiches, and spicily sauced wings are pleasant deviations from the pizza. There are really no bad choices here, but the pizza is truly gold star–worthy.

Rangoon Burmese Restaurant, Chinatown; 112 N. 9th St., Philadelphia, PA 19107; (215) 829-8939; phillychinatown.com; Burmese; $$. In a section of the city replete with Asian restaurants and takeout spots, Burmese cuisine gets lost in the shuffle—so much so that the satisfying crunch of flaky thousand layer bread or bright taste of jungle chicken remains elusive to most. The tea leaf salad may be odd-sounding but is surprisingly pleasant and not at all overwhelming. The apprehensive will find that many of the dishes most closely resemble Chinese fare but are often prepared with a lighter hand. Bowls of noodles and some of the curried offerings will satiate tamer palates but the real adventure lies in savoring dishes like the tender, spicy basil and coriander spiced Burmese spare ribs or the heat-generating red bean squid.

Rotisseur, Rittenhouse Square; 2100-06 S. 21st St., Philadelphia, PA 19103; (215) 496-9494; rotisseur.net; New American/International; $. You wouldn't expect to find a chicken joint (rotisserie or otherwise) in posh Rittenhouse Square, but BYOB Rotisseur puts similar urban outposts to shame with juicy roasted chicken and top-notch sides like succotash and pickled vegetables; those who want to up the healthiness quotient of their meal even further will take comfort in the baked kale chips, sautéed cauliflower and roasted beets with feta. While the restaurant dabbles in international territory a bit with the pesto chicken salad and chicken *bánh mì* (a traditional Vietnamese sandwich), Rotisseur puts its best foot forward with its straightforward comfort food offerings and, honestly, a box of mini corn muffins is just too cute (and tasty) to pass up. Perfect for grabbing a quick after work bite. Closed Sat and Sun.

Sbraga, Avenue of the Arts; 440 S. Broad St., Philadelphia, PA 19146; (215) 735-1913; sbraga.com; New American; $$$. In a world where the popularity of television personalities is as fleeting as the lifespan of a mayfly, it's rare that 15 minutes of TV fame translate to real world success; that is especially true of reality cooking show alums, but *Top Chef* season 7 winner Kevin Sbraga hopes to write a different ending to his reality-show story. Sbraga recently opened his eponymous Broad Street eatery to critical acclaim. In a bold move, he eschews hefty price tags in favor of a $45 prix fixe menu consisting of a starter, fish, meat, and dessert course (additional courses can be ordered a la carte at the bar). Elevating simple and familiar fare seems to be Sbraga's forte with dishes like a savory and surprisingly interesting veal mousse meat loaf getting a smattering of bacon marmalade or light, crispy fish-and-chips perched atop a puddle of curried remoulade and cornichons. The top chef admits he "tastes the dishes constantly and tweaks them all the time." As for his rapidly growing legion of devotees, they welcome the tweaking for it is in those meticulous details that Sbraga's genius is discovered.

Shiao Lan Kung, Chinatown; 930 Race St., Philadelphia, PA 19107; (215) 928-0282; Chinese; $$. This tiny, unassuming Chinatown restaurant is often praised as the best and most authentic in the city. Such real-deal Cantonese favorites as hot and sour soup and oysters in black bean sauce are not to be missed. You absolutely cannot visit without trying the "salt-baked triple," which consists of squid, shrimp, and scallops—even those squeamish about the thought of feasting on squid find this dish irresistible. In a section of town where such eateries are a dime a dozen, Shiao Lan Kung stands out as a clear winner.

Supper, South Street District; 926 South St., Philadelphia, PA 19147; (215) 592-8180; supperphilly.com; New American; $$$. There aren't too many people who call dinner "supper" anymore, but perhaps they should because there's something nostalgic and homey about tucking into elevated comfort food in this farm-to-table restaurant. Busy, eclectic South Street is better known for its plentiful sandwich and pizza shops than its fine-dining offerings, but Supper represents a much-welcomed change. A daily selection of deviled eggs and tasty "lil dixies"—mini Kentucky ham, fried green tomato, and pimiento cheese sliders—hark back to the time of church potluck dinners and gingham picnic blankets. While the crispy duck leg confit and pecan sage waffle with maple bourbon jus is a bit sweet, the duck  waffles serve as a beautiful play on chicken and waffles and are a favorite among patrons. Those craving something more familiar will rejoice in Supper's brisket burger—a half-pound brisket burger ground in-house and topped with caramelized onions, heirloom tomatoes, and Neuske's bacon accompanied by a side of sinfully indulgent duck fat–fried fingerling potatoes. Food like this definitely makes supper the favorite meal of the day.

Talula's Garden, Washington Square West; 210 W. Washington Sq., Philadelphia, PA 19106; (215) 592-7787; talulasgarden.com; New American; $$$. The dining world waited with bated breath for the opening of Aimee Olexy's Philadelphia farm-inspired outpost, mostly because of her impressive résumé and partnership with legendary restaurateur Stephen Starr. (She is also the owner of one-year-reservation-waiting-list Talula's Table in Kennett Square, PA.) Starr is quite the—pardon the pun—star-maker and has a knack for spotting the best and brightest talent and he did not let the Philadelphia dining scene down when he gave the reigns to Olexy and let her work her magic—and magical it is. You can almost taste the individual seasons in notable dishes like tender braised rabbit with handkerchief pasta, pecorino, and fava beans or brioche rolls with ramp butter. If you're a *fromage* lover,
the extensive cheese list is phenomenal
and the waitstaff is very knowledgeable
and accommodating in assisting with
selections. While the menu changes
frequently, Olexy's steadfast commitment to supporting local purveyors and offering fresh, seasonal ingredients remains a constant.

Tashan, Avenue of the Arts; 777 S. Broad St., Philadelphia, PA 19147; (267) 687-2170; mytashan.com; Indian; $$$. For years, Philadelphians have flocked to Indian favorite **Tiffin** (p. 56) to satisfy their curry cravings and newcomer Tashan seeks to change that flow of traffic and, with its upscale trappings and elevated Indian cuisine, it is already a hit among locals. A variety of tandoor are available and perhaps none is tastier than the *paneer shashlik*—a housemade cottage cheese dish that cheekily offers a nod to the City of Brotherly Love with a Philadelphia cream cheese mousseline and black peppercorns. The *aloo tikki*, outstanding variety of *chaat* (Indian street food snacks), Mangalorean sausages, and garlic naan are excellent as is an extensive wine list.

Tria, Rittenhouse Square/Washington Square West; 123 S. 18th St., Philadelphia, PA 19103 and 1137 Spruce St., Philadelphia, PA 19107; (215) 972-8742; triacafe.com; New American; $$. Lucky for wine lovers, craft beer enthusiasts, and cheese aficionados, James Beard Award–winning Tria has two Center City locations along with owner Jon Myerow's other ode-to-oenophiles eatery Tria Wine Room (formerly Biba). Tria is a sleek, modern hipster hangout usually packed to the rafters with refined foodies who are über-knowledgeable about what's on their plates and in their glasses. Perhaps the knowledge is innate, but it is more likely the result of taking a class or two at Tria's "Sunday School"—a fun, interactive weekend class that features a tasting and a lecture on a different wine, cheese, or beer each week. The restaurant's menu is composed of small plates (the popular truffled egg toast with fontina is a rich, buttery delight), salads, and sandwiches with, of course, extensive wine, beer, and cheese lists. For a complete listing of Sunday School classes, visit the restaurant's website; wine and beer tastings are approximately $5 a glass and cheese is about $4 per tasting. Tria also offers classes through its Fermentation School; detailed information is available on the website.

Vedge, Washington Square West; 1221 Locust St., Philadelphia, PA 19107; (215) 320-7500; vedgerestaurant.com; Vegan; $$$. Vegetarian restaurants and their stricter vegan counterparts have often gotten a bad reputation (and sometimes deservedly so) for serving boring, unimaginative food that is nothing more than spruced up salads. Stylishly modern Vedge (formerly vegetarian fave Horizons) breaks through all those restrictive notions and smartly sidesteps the stereotypes with a sexy menu of tapas-style plates of smoked eggplant, cauliflower, and garbanzo beans topped with a punched-up salsa verde; fresh farm vegetables can be ordered from the "dirt list." A steak-spice seared tofu with chanterelles, kabocha squash, and madeira will convince even the staunchest carnivores that a meal needn't include meat to be tasty, and mothers everywhere are justified in encouraging their children to eat their veggies.

Vetri, Washington Square West; 1312 Spruce St., Philadelphia, PA 19107; (215) 732-3478; vetriristorante.com; Italian; $$$$. James Beard Award–winning chef Marc Vetri has been on the radar of food lovers for quite some time. He has garnered serious praise and a cadre of loyal fans for not only Vetri but his other two Philadelphia restaurants as well (**Amis,** p. 71 and **Osteria,** p. 46). However, eponymous Vetri is undoubtedly the crown jewel in his trifecta of eateries—quite simply, it is the restaurant that eventually lands on every gourmand's culinary bucket list. The chef's tasting menu—the sole offering—is an authentic Italian gastronomic feast of the highest order. Be forewarned: You will dine on adeptly prepared dishes like spinach gnocchi in brown butter or tender baby goat with velvety polenta and your dream-like trance will be interrupted only by the promise of a decadent dessert. You will wonder why you don't dine here every night and then you will look in your wallet and be reminded that, at $135 per person, Vetri is—like all indulgences—to be savored and enjoyed sparingly.

Village Whiskey, Rittenhouse Square; 118 S. 20th St., Philadelphia, PA 19103; (215) 665-1088; villagewhiskey.com; New American; $$. Three simple words can sum up Chef-Owner José Garces's casual eatery: duck fat fries. Sure, America has been carrying on a torrid love affair with fries for quite some time but the simple (and ingenious) technique of cooking them in duck fat hoists the humble potato to something so refined that you wonder why you hadn't tried this earlier. As if that is not decadent enough, you can opt to have your fries slathered in Sly Fox cheddar sauce and meltingly tender short rib. Yes, it's a caloric bomb but completely worth a day's calories. With all the talk of the incredible side dishes (the house-made cheese puffs and tater tots are another win), it's almost easy to forget about the burgers. Almost. The burgers are some of the best in the city and, regardless of your disdain for looking too trendy, topping any of the burger selections with a fried egg is an excellent  idea as is ordering a cocktail (or two) from the fun and cheeky drink menu.

Wedge + Fig, Old City; 160 N. 3rd St., Philadelphia, PA 19106; (215) 238-1716; wedgeandfig.com; Traditional American; $$. Everything in this Old City cheese shop, including the title, is an homage to *fromage*. A glass case houses wedges of gruyère, Stilton, cheddar and the like while the grilled cheese "bar" is every cheese aficionado's fantasy. Start off with a sturdy Hudson Bread foundation, choose from a variety of cheeses from the tame to the frou-frou, and choose to either enjoy it as-is or top off all that goodness with a few condiments like caramelized onions, avocado, tomato, or artisanal pickles (which represent only a sampling of available toppers). If you'd rather let the experts in the kitchen work their magic, the menu offers specialty salads, sandwiches, and soups. Something as simple as mac and cheese is transformed with a savory bacon lattice top and a flaky crust and the truffle oil–kissed egg salad with capers and shallots would blow your elementary school, brown-bag egg salad sandwich away.

Xochitl, Society Hill; 408 S. 2nd St., Philadelphia, PA 19147; (215) 238-7280; xochitlphilly.com; Mexican/Late Night; $$$. Society Hill Mexican hotspot Xochitl (pronounced *so-cheet*) traded its once-upscale decor for a more laid-back, less formal feel and the result is a much more relaxed atmosphere and casual menu. Impeccably done standards like pork tacos, *queso fundido* (melted cheese and chorizo), and guacamole made tableside are served alongside more adventurous dishes like *lengua a la vera-cruzana* (a tostada of beef tongue simmered in salsa) and *huitlacoche* flan (a traditional flan made with corn fungus). The restaurant is as popular for its bar as it is its food; an extensive list of cocktails, Spanish wines, and *aguas frescas* is impressive but the real draw is the more than 75 types of tequila served. Xochitl also hosts a popular Sunday brunch with a limited version of their regular menu—*chilaquiles* and a Bloody Maria are a must. In addition to its regular happy hour, Xochitl also offers a late night happy hour in the lounge Thurs to Sat from 10 pm to midnight. See Chef Gabriel Montalvo's recipe for **Huarache de Hongos (Mushroom Flatbread)** on p. 250.

Zahav, Society Hill; 237 St. James Pl., Philadelphia, PA 19106; (215) 625-8800; zahavrestaurant.com; Middle Eastern; $$$. This Society Hill hotspot's name literally means "gold" in Hebrew and that's exactly what popular chef and restaurateur Michael Solomonov has struck with his ode to Israeli cooking. He pulls back the curtain on a cuisine that is still foreign to some and proves to diners that there is more to Middle Eastern food than falafel. Jerusalem street food is reinterpreted, elevated, and prepared with the adroitness of a chef much older than Solomonov; it's hard to believe that the modest chickpea—a staple in Israeli cooking and the key ingredient in hummus—is craftily manipulated and transformed into several varieties of the tahini-spiked spread. A daily selection of eight types of *salatim* (salads) and *shipudim* (skewers of grilled meat—think kebabs) along with an ambitious (but well-executed) meze offering complete the menu. Those looking to sample a traditional Israeli spread would do well to order one of two tastings

Sweet Dreams

Who says college is just for pledging to a rowdy fraternity and throwing all-night keggers? For smarty pants entrepreneur/ owner and UPenn graduate Seth Berkowitz, college was for brainstorming. Like most successful businesses, the concept was simple: deliver hot, delicious cookies to sleepless students and thus **Insomnia Cookies** (108 S. 16th St., Philadelphia, PA 19103, 215-563-7426, insomniacookies.com; and various other locations) was born. Since its inception, the late-night sweet shop has moved beyond the confines of college campuses and expanded its offerings to include brownies and cookie cakes. Though consumption may send you into sugar shock, the popular chocolate chunk and oatmeal raisin varieties often sell out quickly. Decadence comes in the form of jumbo deluxe cookies—be forewarned: the s'mores cookie is habit-forming. It's probably not good for your waistline or diet, but cookies are also available by the dozen or in larger quantities.

from the chef's menu which offers a selection of small dishes. With a staggering amount of vegetable preparations readily available and stretching beyond stereotypical nonmeat dishes, Zahav has become a favorite destination for vegetarians as well.

Post-Midnight Munching

National Mechanics, Old City; 22 S. 3rd St., Philadelphia, PA 19106; (215) 701-4883; nationalmechanics.com; Traditional American/Late Night; $$. The National Mechanics Building has seen many incarnations in its day—among its former uses, it's been a bank, church, and nightclub and has endured more than one fire. Thankfully, the imposing stone building has survived and, for years, has housed one of the friendliest pubs in the city. Feeling like having a drink and grabbing some late-night munchies? Two words: Bacon vodka. This is just one of the quirky items found on the menu at this Old City pub that offers nostalgic and innovative food alike. Old-school delights like corn dogs and tomato soup and grilled cheese are comforting but if you really want to go the comfort food extreme, try the "Frito Taco Extravaganza"—a ripped-open bag of the corn chip snack favorite topped with chili and cheese. All that food has to be washed down with something, right? With 32 varieties of beer gracing the roster, you can quench your thirst in one place without having to bar hop.

Nodding Head Brewery & Restaurant, Rittenhouse Square; 1516 Sansom St., Philadelphia, PA 19102; (215) 569-9525; noddinghead.com; New American/Late Night; $$. Hidden in plain sight in the heart of Center City, this brewery has gained a loyal following of beer lovers and foodies alike. Serving large portions without the hefty price tag is the hallmark of this local hotspot and definitely

a draw for the hungry late-night set. Burgers are juicy and bolstered by local ingredients and the ale-soaked Moroccan mussels with mint, cinnamon, and garlic honey are the perfect blend of sweet and savory. Drinkers flock here in droves to enjoy creative, in-house brewed beers and Nodding Head definitely does not come up short in the beer-naming department. Monkey Knife Fight may conjure up images of dueling primates, but at Nodding Head it refers to a tasty lemongrass- and ginger-infused beer that has come to be the most popular beer on tap.

The QUICK FIXX, South Street District; 1511 South St., Philadelphia, PA 19146; (267) 273-1066; thequickfixx.com; Italian/ Late Night; $. See listing on p. 91.

Xochitl, Society Hill; 408 S. 2nd St., Philadelphia, PA 19147; (215) 238-7280; xochitlphilly.com; Mexican/Late Night; $$$. See listing on p. 100.

Specialty Stores, Markets & Producers

La Colombe, Rittenhouse Square; 130 S. 19th St., Philadelphia, PA 19103; (215) 563-0860; lacolombe.com; Coffee Shop; $. Plenty of places around the city have menus that boast La Colombe coffee but if you want the true experience of whole-roasted beans and friendly, knowledgeable baristas, head to this Rittenhouse Square flagship location. La Colombe has built its business partly on its steadfast commitment to its fair trade practices and partly on its excellent variety of custom-blended coffee. This place has a fierce following and an empty table is precious real estate so snagging a seat to drink your coffee and zone out with your headphones may prove difficult. Whether or not you're able to get a seat, an inexpensive cappuccino or a rich espresso drink is a good bet, and there are plenty of pastries, treats, and bags of coffee for sale. Take care not to mistake this coffee shop for other frou-frou places that offer flavorings and various stir-ins—it's all about the coffee here.

Old Nelson Food Company, Market East; 701 Chestnut St., Philadelphia, PA 19176; (215) 627-7090; oldnelsonfood.com; Specialty Market/Deli; $. In a section of the city that desperately needs a place like Old Nelson, think of this place as an upscale convenience store that offers one-stop shopping to busy commuters and residents. Without having to set foot in an actual supermarket, shoppers can pick up specialty items, but ticking off everything on your grocery list is not recommended—the tab adds up quickly here, thanks in part to the fact that you're paying for convenience. The deli has surprisingly good sandwiches made with Boar's Head deli meats so you're in for a high-quality treat when ordering a turkey hoagie or a good old-fashioned ham sandwich; the salads offer an even healthier option. The business crowd descends on Old Nelson at lunchtime, so calling in your order ahead is a wise choice. Washington Square Park is nearby, which, weather permitting, makes a perfect lunch spot.

Sook Hee's Produce & Squeeze Juice Bar, Penn Center; 1701 John F. Kennedy Blvd., Philadelphia, PA 19103; (215) 568-2834; themarketatcomcastcenter.com; Produce/Juice Bar; $$. Nestled inside the Comcast Center and part of its market, Sook Hee's provides a Technicolor array of produce—rows of fresh fruit and veggies can be found throughout the store. Fresh salads, a variety of healthy snacks and a tricked-out juice bar make this place a premier lunch destination. Sidle up to the juice bar and order one of the concoctions from the menu or channel your inner health nut and mix and match from fresh fruit and vegetable options and have the barista blend it for you. The juices tend to run on the pricey side—especially if you choose your own ingredients—but provide a great alternative to typical lead-belly lunches.

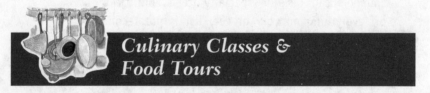

Culinary Classes & Food Tours

Italian Market Tour, Meeting places vary (check web site for details); (215) 280-3746; italianmarketphilly.org. A walk through

the storied Italian Market and surrounding neighborhood—led by a
longtime merchant—allows participants to get up close and
personal with the market's vendors. The Italian Market is the
oldest and largest 7-day open-
air market in the nation and a
foodie's dream. Don't count this tour

out as yet another scripted, run-of-the-mill excursion. The tour
guide regales the group with stories about the market's colorful history and its cast of even more colorful characters. Between rounds
of hilarious anecdotes, participants are treated to a sampling of
bites from the market's most iconic food vendors. Those looking for
a solo experience are able to take a self-guided tour with narration
available for download. Guided tours are available by appointment
only; visit the website for specifics.

La Cucina at the Market, Market East; 11th & Arch Streets,
Philadelphia, PA 19107; (215) 922-1170; lacucinaatthemarket.com.
Reading Terminal Market is often described as the Holy Grail of
the buy-local food movement in Philadelphia and, in addition to a
number of vendors, it also boasts its own cooking space. Offering a
few classes a month, Chef-Owner Anna Maria Florio and her instructors teach cooking classes that utilize fresh ingredients from the
market to teach 1-day courses ranging from how to craft the perfect
soup to how to sharpen your knife skills. The classes are relaxed and

WHAT THE TRUCK?

In general, Philadelphia is a fast-paced city full of serious eaters, and the culinary scene has adapted to keep pace with lifestyles of an on-the-go population. Food trucks, mobile carts, and even tricked-out tricycles have become de rigueur all over the city—you'll find them camped out near university campuses, idling on the corners of the business district, and dishing up great street eats in local parks. Although a few proprietors have actual brick-and-mortar locations with traditional contact information, many mobile eateries utilize social media to broadcast their location, menu changes, and specials. But remember, most food trucks are cash-only so give your plastic a break and make sure you hit the ATM before hopping in line.

Comfort food—more specifically, soul food—is enjoying a comeback and **Denise's Soul Food** (30th & Market Streets, 215-424-7022), **Jamaican D's** (1700 Spring Garden St., 215-668-5909) and Vendy Award (annual food truck awards) winner **GiGi and Big R's Caribbean Soul Food** (38th & Spruce Streets, 610-389-2150) specialize in Caribbean and American soul food. Jerk chicken, rice and beans, and a slew of side dishes are popular.

Most people know tacos are the perfect street food—portable, tasty, and conducive to eating on the go. Several food truck operators are catching on to the taco craze as well, finding ways to stuff just about anything into a tortilla shell—from spicy pulled pork to cheesesteak-style rib eye. **Taco Loco** (S. 4th Street & Washington Avenue), **Tacos Don Memo** (3800 Sansom St.; @tacosdonmemo) and Vendy Award People's Choice winner **Cucina Zapata** (31st Street & Ludlow Street; @Cucina_Zapata) are also dishing up delicious tacos around the city.

City-dwellers also have an affinity for Middle Eastern food as well, and **Falafel Truck** (NE corner 20th & Market Streets) and

King of Falafel (S. 16th Street & JFK Boulevard) battle for falafel supremacy in busy Center City. The decision seems to be split when it comes to choosing a favorite—both serve extremely tasty food. However, the owner of Falafel Truck has made a name for himself with his no-nonsense service that can come off as brusque if you aren't familiar with the ordering process. The only choice you'll get is "chicken" or "no chicken"—referring to the enormous falafel platters.

    The Dapper Dog (2nd & Poplar Streets; 203-887-8813; thedapperdog.org; @thedapperdog) and **Renaissance Sausage** (renaissancesausage.com; @TheSausageTruck) have figured out a way

to dish up dogs and sausages with a twist. The Dapper Dog, much to the delight of midnight munchers, is open ridiculously late; check the website and Twitter for updates.

    For the health-conscious and those seeking lighter fare, **Fresh Fruit Truck** (37th & Spruce Streets) is a great option that serves fresh-cut fruit and smoothies (they are not advertised but can be made). **Produce Truck** (43rd & Walnut Streets) is a produce stand on wheels and an excellent alternative to a traditional grocery store and much lighter on the wallet as well.

    Just about everyone loves an ice cream truck, but what about an ice cream tricycle? **Little Baby's Ice Cream** (littlebabysicecream .com; @LittleBabysIC) specializes in artisanal ice cream in creative flavors like Earl Grey sriracha and birch beer vanilla bean. If more traditional sweets are your thing, **Sweet Box Cupcakes** (1600 John F. Kennedy Blvd.; 215-237-4647; @SweetBoxTruck) and **Sugar Philly Truck** (38th & Walnut Streets; 267-940-7473; sugarphillytruck.com; @sugarphilly) often sell out of their decadent cupcakes and *macarons* respectively.

approachable and feel much more like spending time in a home kitchen than a stuffy classroom. The fact that La Cucina is located within one of the busiest (and most popular) markets in the country often inspires students to pick up some groceries from one of the many vendors so they can whip up their own meals at home.

Philly on Tap, (215) 280-3746; philadelphiaurbanadventures .com. The 2-hour walking tour, one of the many options offered by Philadelphia Urban Adventures, will take you to the city's most eclectic watering holes to sip the city's finest beers—all during happy hour. Novices and hops aficionados alike will appreciate learning about the brewing process and the city's longstanding brewing culture.

Rolling Barrel, (610) 292-0880; rollingbarrel.com. Rolling Barrel is one of the latest establishments to offer culinary tours. Led by two craft beer enthusiasts who have built a successful business by offering pairing events and hosting educational pub crawls, the instructive tours have garnered praise around the city. The walking tour lasts approximately five hours and leads beer lovers to four bars while answering the age-old question on the lips of every diehard hops head: "Where can I find the best beer in the city?" The duo introduces participants to their favorite neighborhoods and pulls back the curtain on the city's best bars where bar owners are up for discussions and demonstrations and happily pour samples. The only downside is the fact that the tours operate rather infrequently—currently offered only three times a year.

Tippler's Tour, Old City; 6th and Chestnut Streets, Philadelphia, PA 19106; (215) 629-4026; historicphiladelphia.org. Beer ye! Beer ye! Tippler's Tour is the perfect tour for libation lovers and history buffs alike. Led by a tour guide bedecked in colonial attire, it is an often raucous and hilarious colonial pub crawl through historic Philadelphia that makes stops at some of Philadelphia's finest bars, taverns, and breweries. Participants are given a small handbook from which they can learn authentic pub lingo and the all-important "Huzzah!"—the way Ben Franklin himself would have properly toasted someone in his heyday. Notable stops include a visit to historical **City Tavern** (p. 66), Triumph Brewing Company, and **National Mechanics** (p. 103). Sips include local favorite Yards Philadelphia Pale Ale, Strongbow hard cider, and a pink Champagne cocktail crafted from an 18th-century recipe; cornmeal-dusted calamari, savory meat pies, and chicken skewers serve as perfect foils.

Tria Fermentation School, Rittenhouse Square; 1601 Walnut St., Ste. 620, Philadelphia, PA 19176; (215) 972-7076; triacafe .com. Known for its delicious small plates, hip crowd, and knowledgeable staff, Tria Fermentation School is an oenophile's dream destination. The swank formal classroom is a spin-off of the eponymous restaurant/wine bar and offers informative wine classes and food pairings to students eager to learn more about oenology. Sip by sip, participants can learn how to find the perfect Pinot Grigio or how to scout out inexpensive bottles of vino from traditionally expensive wine appellations like Barolo and Amarone. Students will leave each class with a list of the wines consumed in class and a handy guide for finding them around town. For those who like to mix it up a bit, Tria's Sunday School class offers a beer, wine, and cheese pairing for a nominal fee per tasting. The sips and bites are perfectly complementary and come with an extensive lesson on provenance, tasting notes, and the like.

Williams-Sonoma, Rittenhouse Square; 200 S. Broad St., Philadelphia, PA 19102; (215) 545-7392; williams-sonoma.com. Considered by many to be the Valhalla of cookware and kitchen tools, the posh Rittenhouse Square location offers a pretty impressive roster of culinary classes in which participants can learn about global cuisine and local foods as well from culinary experts and classically trained chefs. Each class lasts approximately 90 minutes to 2 hours and allows students to get up close and personal with the instructor in the demonstration portion of the class; they are also encouraged to generously sample the featured dish and receive printed copies of the menu to take home. There are also a number of complimentary hour-long cooking technique classes and each is dedicated to a specific culinary topic such as cookware, kitchen tools, or how to incorporate seasonal produce into everyday cooking. Bibliophiles and cookbook collectors should consider the Cookbook Club—a monthly gathering led by the store's talented staff that showcases recipes from a different cookbook every month. Occasionally, the cookbook's author has been known to make a special appearance; past guests have included Food Network's Giada De Laurentiis.

The Wine School of Philadelphia (and The Beer School), Rittenhouse Square; 127 S. 22nd St., Philadelphia, PA 19103; (800) 817-7351; vinology.com. Founder and expert oenophile Keith Wallace and his crack team of instructors offer a host of wine classes, tastings, and food pairings for everyone from vino novices to sommeliers looking to expand their palates. The informative classes are relaxed and casual and feel more like a dinner table chat with a professional sommelier than a structured class. If you are looking for something more official, The Wine School is the only institution (outside of a university) that offers professional wine certification coupled with an independently developed curriculum. Hops enthusiasts will appreciate the beer classes which offer instruction ranging from the basics of brewing to the popular "hopology" class.

Wok 'n Walk, Chinatown; 1010 Cherry St., Philadelphia, PA 19107; (215) 928-9333; josephpoon.com. To some, the thought of navigating the crowded, colorful, and sometimes foreign Chinatown area is daunting to say the least, but the always exuberant Chef

Joseph Poon allays those fears with his fun and educational walking tours. Featured on *The Ellen DeGeneres Show* and *The Tonight Show with Jay Leno*, the tour offers some insight into the cuisine and culture of the lively community. Starting off at Chef Kitchen, Poon's personal cooking space, the tour includes stops at a fortune cookie factory, a Chinese herbal medicine shop, a Chinese place of worship, a Chinese bakery, an Asian grocery store, and a fish market.

South & Southwest

Angora, Bella Vista, Graduate Hospital, Grays Ferry, Italian Market, Newbold, Pennsport, Point Breeze, Queen Village, South Philadelphia, Southwark, Southwest Philadelphia

Though it abuts affluent Center City, South Philadelphia is sort of an everyman part of the city composed of several blue-collar neighborhoods. Thanks to its largely Italian-American population, there is no shortage of "red gravy" restaurants that have come to serve as symbols of the city itself. Throw a stone and you're likely to hit a pizzeria or Italian eatery and for that diners are grateful as the place is teeming with eateries where tomato pie, stromboli, cannoli, and hoagies are bound to make an appearance on the menu. Don't dismiss this area as a one-horse town—there are many cuisines represented within its borders. Over the years, an influx of immigrants has boosted South Philadelphia's dining scene and given way to a whole new notion about what to expect in this area. Most notably, Mexican taquerias and Vietnamese pho eateries have done much to add diversity to its roster of restaurants. Make no mistake, though—South Philly is still the place to go when you're jonesing for zeppole or authentic regional Italian cuisine.

Landmarks

Geno's Steaks, South Philadelphia; 1219 S. 9th St., Philadelphia, PA 19147; (215) 389-0659; genosteaks.com; Traditional American/ Cheesesteaks; $. Steeped in tradition, Geno's has been a South Philly staple for over 45 years. The neon-lit attraction is a 24/7 operation that sits diagonally across the street from its longtime rival—Pat's King of Steaks. Geno's boasts sliced rib-eye cheesesteaks versus the chopped meat variety of its nemesis. The Hatfield-McCoy-like rivalry is the stuff of legends and the topic of sandwich supremacy is a hotly debated subject even among longtime residents. Given its reputation for brusque (which may be putting it mildly) service, knowing how to order properly is key or expect to get a swift lesson. Steaks are ordered from a separate window than sodas and fries and, though it may be acceptable at other cheesesteak places, never order a "whiz wit" (see "How to 'Speak Philly,'" p. 8) here. Its outspoken owner, the late Joey Vento, became known more for his politics than his cheesesteaks and, while some disagree with his opinions, very few deny this eatery its landmark status.

Melrose Diner, South Philadelphia; 1501 Snyder Ave., Philadelphia, PA 19145; (215) 467-6644; Traditional American/

Diner; $. "Everyone one who knows . . . goes to Melrose!" Those old enough to remember Melrose's early days recognize the old jingle that used to serve as the landmark diner's tagline. The shiny, neon-lit hotspot rose to fame with its solid menu of comfort food, snappy waitresses, and a stellar on-site bakery (responsible for its famous butter cookies). Over the years, the 24-hour diner has lured diverse crowds of families, college students, and those nursing hangovers who have found comfort in the homey breakfasts and homemade dinners. Many a South Philadelphia birthday party has been outfitted with one of the decadent buttercream-iced cakes and countless family dinners have been capped off with their mile-high banana cream pie. The retro decor solidified its reputation as an authentic diner and crowded booths once stood as a testament to its popularity. Admittedly, since management has changed and a remodeling has modernized the interior, the diner has lost some of its former luster and largely owes its survival to nostalgia and the hope of locals that it will, once again, return to the glory of its heyday. However, despite its missteps, Melrose is a veritable neighborhood landmark that still offers bright spots and sparks that little feeling of nostalgia for yesteryear.

Pat's King of Steaks, South Philadelphia; 1237 E. Passyunk Ave., Philadelphia, PA 19147; (215) 468-1546; patskingofsteaks.com; Traditional American/Cheesesteaks; $. Founded by the former hot dog-slinging Olivieri brothers in 1930, Pat's engrained itself into the fabric of South Philadelphia food culture right from the beginning. The landmark also asserts its place in history as being the inventor of the now-famous cheesesteak (see p. 4) and the chopped meat-style of the iconic sandwich is the perfect contrast to that of competitor Geno's Steaks. Pat's does share a similarity with its neon-bright neighbor—the strict ordering method. A posted sign reminds customers to have cash in hand, their order ready to go, and to know the proper ordering method or be forced to head to the back of the line. This is the perfect place to practice your "Philly talk"; it's perfectly acceptable here to order a "whiz wit" (see "How to 'Speak Philly,'" p. 8). World renowned Pat's and Geno's draw huge crowds of tourists and loyalists and both eateries offer canopy-style outdoor seating—making people-watching or cheesesteak-debating all the more entertaining.

Foodie Faves

Al Zaytouna, Italian Market; 906 Christian St., Philadelphia, PA 19147; (215) 574-5040; al-zaytouna.com; Middle Eastern; $. A certain level of defiance is needed to open a Middle Eastern restaurant in the middle of the Italian Market—thank goodness for rebellion. Al Zaytouna turns out expertly prepared *foul* (a traditional fava bean dip), stuffed grape leaves, and *lebneh* along with a bevy of salads and kebabs; chicken shawarma is a good choice as well. If the sandwich menu looks familiar, it's because most of the entrees are transformed into a more portable version. For a departure from the usual, try the *merguez,* which is a blend of spicy ground beef and lamb served on a baguette topped with french fries.

American Sardine Bar, Point Breeze; 1801 Federal St., Philadelphia, PA 19146; (215) 215-2152; american sardinebar.com; New American; $$. Imagine a place where you and a group of your rabble-rousing cohorts can grab a few beers, get great grub, and not spend the equivalent of a mortgage payment. This Point Breeze sandwich beacon is a relative newcomer, but it already feels like a  cozy neighborhood staple—an impressive feat to achieve by such a huge bar. The bi-level bar offers an impressive, meticulously curated 16 beers on tap downstairs with more refined options being offered on the 2nd floor. As far as the menu goes, there's no doubt the sandwich reigns supreme here. From the open-faced roasted chicken sandwich with buttery toast, mashed potatoes, savory mushrooms, and gravy that would rival your grandmother's, to the delicious breakfast take on the cheesesteak, this newly minted gem is one of the best things to happen to Point Breeze since sliced bread.

Ants Pants Cafe, Graduate Hospital; 2212 South St., Philadelphia, PA 19146; (215) 875-8002; antspantscafe.com; Traditional

American; $$. This diminutive cafe offers a menu of big flavors and a host of crowd pleasers. Breakfast and brunch are a big deal at this place and Ants Pants puts its best foot forward with delicious morning starters like crème brûlée french toast with sour cream sauce or the popular dill scrambled eggs with feta. The lunch menu is executed in the same simple and delicious manner with a smattering of sandwiches and salads like the roasted red pepper sandwich with avocado and pesto or the spinach salad with goat cheese and green apples. Your best bet would be to arrive for breakfast as the crowd begins to swell during brunch hours and service tends to be rushed and a tad aloof. Cash only.

Balkan Express Restaurant, Graduate Hospital; 2237 Grays Ferry Ave., Philadelphia, PA 19146; (215) 545-1255; balkanexpressres taurant.com; Mediterranean/Hungarian; $$. Simple, rustic fare is where this family-owned BYOB shines. A few smoked meat dishes, along with salads, stews, and soups make up the limited menu and offer insight into Balkan cuisine. If you're unfamiliar with the cooking style and food of this region, it borrows from many surrounding cultures and doesn't differ too greatly from that of the Mediterranean. Start off with a cucumber salad then move on to the lamb steak or stuffed cabbage. The *muckalicka*—tender cubes of slow-cooked beef with peppers, onions, and tomatoes—showcase vegetables that are grown by the husband-and-wife owners in their off-site garden. Before succumbing to a full belly, try the baklava and a cup of the notoriously strong Turkish coffee.

Bibou, Bella Vista; 1009 S. 8th St., Philadelphia, PA 19147; (215) 965-8290; biboubyob.com; French; $$$. When Robert Parker, the world's most renowned wine critic, offers his seal of approval by dubbing an eatery "the best French bistro in the country," you can guarantee that the restaurant is something special. Indeed, 30-seater Bibou was the recipient of such lavish praise and it is every bit as special as the accolades would imply. On any given night, the dining room is filled to the rafters with patrons who have made their reservations a month or two in advance. By far, the most popular dish here is the stuffed bone marrow which sounds simplistic but is prepared so exquisitely, it almost defies explanation. Presented on the half bone, the preparation permits the marrow to liquefy and infuse the stuffing with rich flavor. It is served with a humble potato and green salad—it's highly likely that anything more sophisticated than that would send one's palate into sensory overload. A *pied de porc,* or pig's foot, is stuffed with decadent, silken *foie gras* and served atop French lentils. Of course, such an indulgent meal warrants relinquishing all restraint so ordering the lavender-tinged crème brûlée is not only acceptable but highly encouraged.

Bistrot La Minette, Queen Village; 623 S. 6th St., Philadelphia, PA 19147; (215) 925-8000; bistrotlaminette.com; French; $$$. Chef Peter Woolsey's classic French bistro fare is served in this beautifully appointed neighborhood charmer with a menu focused not on reinventing the wheel but using quality ingredients to craft traditional French dishes. His return from his yearly trek to France is always a highly anticipated affair as inspired dishes are sure to show up on the menu. The *tarte paysanne,* a rustic tomato tart with mustard and crème fraîche feels homey and comforting and is plated with a simple frisée salad. Pan-seared duck breast with grilled white asparagus and potato confit forgoes the usual cherry accompaniment and is served with a rich black-currant sauce instead. In addition to offering a sophisticated brunch on the weekends, a well-executed French menu and a doting staff are reminders that a plane ticket to Paris need not be purchased to experience *les petits plaisirs.*

Bitar's, Bella Vista; 947 Federal St., Philadelphia, PA 19147; (215) 755-1121; bitars.com; Middle Eastern; $. Part grocery store/part eatery, this often overlooked little jewel is the neighborhood's best-kept secret, but it's a near certainty that once you sample the inexpensive eats here, you'll be hooked. In terms of prepared foods, you'll find all the usual suspects—fresher than fresh *fattoush,* tabouleh, crispy falafel, and a pretty extensive selection of gyros round out the menu. For larger parties and appetites, there's even a catering menu. Can't get enough of the in-house Middle Eastern delights? There's a grocery store stocked with traditional ingredients and goods, so make sure to stock up on homemade pita, eggplant dip, and imported feta.

Catahoula, Queen Village; 775 S. Front St., Philadelphia, PA 19147; (215) 271-9300; catahoularestaurant.com; Creole/Cajun; $$. A few concepts have done stints in the space this unexpected Creole eatery now occupies, but if public opinion is any indication,

Catahoula won't be going anywhere anytime soon. On most nights, the place is largely filled with neighborhood residents who slurp oysters on the half shell with green Tabasco mignonette, sip spoonsful of dark-hued Acadian gumbo and revel in plates of andouille sausage–studded duck jambalaya. A selection of po' boys, a few preparations of shrimp, and soulful étouffée make an appearance on the N'awlins-inspired menu. Authentic Abita beer, a limited wine menu, and an array of Bourbon Street–style cocktails complement the menu of comforting classics.

Circles Contemporary Asian Cafe, Newbold; 1514 Tasker Ave., Philadelphia, PA 19145; (267) 687-1778; circlesnewbold.com; Thai; $$. The slightly garish bright green–paneled storefront usually causes first time visitors to check their GPS devices. With its lone bulletproof glass–paned takeout window, second thoughts are understandable, but don't judge a book by its cover just yet—the actual dining room is across the street and does much to allay the fears of the timid. Don't give all the credit to the decor— Chef-Owner Alex Boonphaya's creations are helping to resurrect Philadelphia's somewhat anemic Thai cuisine landscape. Kabocha pumpkin curry laced with fresh Thai basil and the shrimp drunken noodles are among the most satisfying dishes, and who knew tofu and corn could coincide so delightfully as they do in the deep-fried fritters that are served with a warm crab and tomato broth? Turn up the heat with the *pad kaprow,* whose spice level can be adjusted simply by requesting the "Thai hot" version.

Cochon, Queen Village; 801 E. Passyunk Ave., Philadelphia, PA 19147; (215) 923-7675; cochonbyob.com; French; $$$. In the "red gravy district"—a section of the city saturated with Italian eateries, Cochon is an anomaly—a French restaurant that expertly plies its haute cuisine trade in a decidedly meat and potatoes part of town. The weathered exterior belies the succinct and sophisticated menu, where duck *magret* with *haricots verts* and sweet potato puree and slow-cooked suckling pig topped with a flawless poached egg and served with lentils and charred brussels sprouts are the highlights. During Sunday brunch, when a waiter suggests eggs *cochon,* be wise and heed the advice—the tender pulled pork atop a bacon-studded gruyère biscuit with poached eggs and a rich Mornay sauce is well worth relinquishing your decision-making authority. Cash only. Closed Mon.

Dante & Luigi's, Bella Vista; 762 S. 10th St., Philadelphia, PA 19147; (215) 922-9501; danteandluigis.com; Italian; $$. Be careful when referring to this neighborhood staple as a "hit"—it was actually the site of a notorious mob hit back in the late '80s. Normally, that kind of dubious honor would have shuttered a restaurant immediately, but South Philadelphians don't scare that easily and, besides, the food is too good to let this place sleep with the fishes. This is authentic Italian at its finest; eggplant rollatini and the diet-breaking rigatoni carbonara conjure up memories of Sunday dinners around the family table. Heartier appetites may prefer the classic osso buco or the signature perciatelli Genovese—pasta tossed in a white wine and cream-tinged veal Bolognese; a respectable list of Italian wines make for the perfect complement. If sipping vino with your meal isn't enough, try one of the boozy confections from the dessert menu before throwing in the towel—Italian rum cake and the Amaretto-infused ricotta cheesecake are heavenly.

Evangel Temple Church of Deliverance, Southwest Philadelphia; 1407 S. 49th St., Philadelphia, PA 19143; (215) 729-2581; Soul Food; $$. Dedicated church ladies are on a mission to save souls with . . . well, soul food at this church-cum-food tent. On Friday and Saturday nights, the ladies don old-school nurses' uniforms and set up shop on the church's sidewalk and line up behind a row of tables and chafing dishes nearly a half a block long, serving platters of saucy ribs, oxtail and lima beans, smoky ham hocks, chicken and dumplings, and a score of standards from the soul food playbook until about 2 a.m. They're right back at it bright and early on Sunday morning as they take their operation indoors and serve from the church's kitchen to catch the after-church crowd looking to fill their bellies and feed their souls. If you're feeling especially sinful, make sure to grab a slice of their sweet potato pie.

Falone's Luncheonette, Southwest Philadelphia; 7337 Elmwood Ave., Philadelphia, PA 19142; (215) 365-7445; Traditional American/Sandwiches; $$. Unless you live in the neighborhood, you may have yet to discover Falone's; the little lunch spot suffers from a bit of a location problem. It's buried deep in a residential area, but it serves one of the juiciest cheesesteaks in the city and, at a respectable size and priced under $6, it makes for a great lunchtime find; the staff is super-friendly and always willing to fill a rush order for those on the go. The menu itself is classic luncheonette—sandwiches, hoagies, and wings; no surprises but enjoyable nonetheless. Because of its close proximity to the airport, Falone's is perfect for travelers who want to take a piece of Philly back home.

Famous 4th Street Delicatessen, Queen Village; 700 S. 4th St., Philadelphia, PA 19147; (215) 922-3274; famous4thstreet delicatessen.com; Deli; $$. Their tagline should be: Even New Yorkers will be impressed, because anyone who has been in the presence of a New Yorker for more than 5 minutes has had to endure a soapbox rant about the assumed superiority of their city's bagels and delis. Famous 4th Street Delicatessen may very well be the deli to dispel all those rumors and quell the bravado. When dining in, a bowl of complimentary pickles is given and the top-quality sandwiches are divided into two sizes—"regular" and "zaftig" (a polite way of saying your sandwich will tower 12 inches above your plate)—and come with a pretty substantial price tag which isn't so hefty considering you'll get about three to four meals out of one sandwich. Traditional favorites like stuffed cabbage and roasted chicken are the ultimate comfort foods and, at the end of the meal, a chocolate chip cookie is presented with your bill.

Federal Donuts, Pennsport; 1219 S. 2nd St., Philadelphia, PA 19147; (267) 687-8258; federaldonuts.com; Korean/Doughnuts; $. Sure, Nobel prizes are hard to come by but whoever first thought of pairing Korean fried chicken and doughnuts is deserving of the coveted award. The unlikely duo of crispy, twice-fried bird and an array of outrageously flavored doughnuts attracts huge crowds to this South Philly newcomer daily. The succinct menu of crispy chicken in zaatar and harissa flavors, glazed chicken in chile-garlic or honey-ginger varieties, and a handful of doughnut variations is mouthwatering—so much so that food is consistently sold out. Once you've experienced the crunch of the sweet and savory honey-ginger chicken followed by the tang of the house-made pickles and the unique combination of raspberry and balsamic or grapefruit and brown sugar in one of the "fancy" dough- nuts, you'll understand why camping out an hour before opening time or being completely content with being packed into diminutive confines like cattle aren't such off-the-wall ideas.

Fond, Queen Village; 1617 E. Passyunk Ave., Philadelphia, PA 19147; (215) 551-5000; fondphilly.com; New American; $$$. Reservations are highly recommended for this tiny Passyunk BYOB or else you risk missing out on remarkably done new American fare. Having worked in arguably one of the best kitchens in Philadelphia, **Le Bec-Fin** (p. 69) alum Lee Styer transforms the most modest ingredients into divine dishes. Pork belly has enjoyed a long run as one of the most favored menu items at area restaurants and at Fond, the love affair with the fat-streaked meat continues as the chef showcases the slow-braised wonder with a sweet/savory salt-and-sugar cure; a crispy sear of pork skin, along with a side of Okinawan sweet potatoes, takes it over the top. Also noteworthy are the veal sweetbreads and beef short ribs with caramelized onion spaetzle and Bordelaise sauce.

Francoluigi's Pizzeria & High Note Cafe, Newbold; 1549 S. 13th St., Philadelphia, PA 19147; (215) 755-8900; francoluigis.com; Italian/Pizza; $$. First things first, don't be confused by the 2-in-1 setup; one side houses a casual pizza joint while the other side—well, the other side presents quite a show. At any other establishment, if your server spontaneously burst into song (opera no less), you'd probably be inclined to promptly ask for the check and back away slowly, but here it's de rigueur and part of the kitsch. Musical theatrics aside, Francoluigi's is one of the most underrated establishments in the city but the pizza here holds its own against (and oftentimes surpasses) more frequented spots and offers a tomato pie to die for. A lengthy sandwich menu dishes up well-executed standards like chicken parm and sausage and peppers. Heartier appetites should opt for something from the entree menu where many of the pastas as well as the gnocchi are served in a divine blush cream sauce that may induce serious plate licking.

Gooey Looie's, Pennsport; 231 McClellan St., Philadelphia, PA 19148; (215) 334-7668; Deli; $. A weathered strip-mall location, cramped environs, and an antiquated cash-only policy usually sound a death knell for a business, but South Philadelphians continue to flock to Gooey Looie's for one thing and one thing only: delicious and enormous sandwiches. Even the chicken salad here is a winner, but the cheesesteaks are the obvious draw. Housed in an impossibly tiny convenience store and often shadowed by the popularity of the more touristy cheesesteak joints, Gooey's has been quietly building a following of die-hard fans for years with its near-perfect sandwich offerings. A sturdy roll gets mounted with a heap of steak and real cheese—not the faux, neon orange "whiz" used in many sandwich shops around the city. Beware when ordering, though, as a sign warns that all sandwiches are presumed to be large unless otherwise specified; ordering a small sandwich here could very well feed a multitude or small village.

Grace Tavern, Grays Ferry; 2229 Grays Ferry Ave., Philadelphia, PA 19146; (215) 893-9580; gracetavern.com; Traditional American/ Pub; $$. If Grace Tavern were a movie, it would be a sleeper hit. In other words, it's the kind of unassuming place that instantly earns your respect once you've had the pleasure of getting your grub (or drink) on here. The blackened green beans with spicy aioli, a popular cult favorite, make the perfect starter before easing into the mushroom and sharp cheddar–topped Kennett Square burger. A broad beer list and a menu of well-prepared

standards satiate both drinkers and diners alike and the laid-back atmosphere inspires that kind of lazy lounging with friends that is the hallmark of any good weekend.

Indonesia Restaurant, Southwest Philadelphia; 1725 Snyder Ave., Philadelphia, PA 19145; (215) 829-1400; loveindonesiarestaurant.com; Indonesian; $$. If you know where to look, the city has a number of Indonesian restaurants and, although sniffing them out may be a bit of a task, that's half the fun. The other half of the fun lies in delighting your palate with satays, curries, noodles and *lumpia*—all of which are found on this eatery's menu. While the generic naming of the restaurant would suggest an equally bland menu, the food here is anything but—you'll find a mix of Indonesian and Javanese fare on the menu. Start off with the *martabak*—a fried ground beef, vegetable, and onion mixture—then ease into a tender lamb satay or one of the noodle dishes. The staff is always willing to make suggestions and it would be wise to heed their advice or else miss out on some excellent bites.

Izumi, South Philadelphia; 1601 E. Passyunk Ave., Philadelphia, PA 19148; (215) 271-1222; izumiphilly.com; Japanese; $$. In a section

of the city that is known for its "red gravy" restaurants, Izumi is a welcome change. A tad more upscale than the usual sushi spots, this place gets bonus points for serving unusual, creative selections. The sashimi platter and spicy tuna roll as well as most of the extensive menu are knockouts, but don't dismiss the cooked fare like the popular rock shrimp tempura with wasabi aioli. Cramped seating and the slightly elevated prices are easily forgiven thanks to a friendly, knowledgeable waitstaff and a killer menu.

Joey Joe's Prime Meats & Deli, South Philadelphia; 1500 McKean St., Philadelphia, PA 19145; (215) 389-4875; Deli; $. Joey Joe's may be stuck in a time warp—the good kind. Tucked away in South Philly, it is an unpretentious deli and market that's been serving up meatball sandwiches, hoagies, and an assortment of sides and salads for over 25 years. Heartier classics like veal scaloppine and lasagna are delicious and comforting in that "you'll-need-a-nap-afterwards" kind of way. Of course you can't take a trip to South Philly without sampling a "saw-seeg" (sausage)—a classic sweet sausage and hot pepper sandwich. As the name implies, the restaurant also offers a variety of butchered meats and "heat and eat" food trays in the event you want to enjoy the Joey Joe's experience at home.

Kennett, Queen Village; 848 S. 2nd St., Philadelphia, PA 19147; (267) 687-1426; kennettrestaurant.com; New American/Gastropub; $$. You'll get an education here whether you want one or not; the unsolicited spiel about the provenance of the menu's ingredients may be a little off-putting to some, but all is quickly forgiven once the food begins rolling out of the kitchen. Small sharing plates, charcuterie, and cheese preparations, burgers, and wood-fired pizzas as well a few sandwiches and mains make up the menu.

The ingredients may have an impressive pedigree, but they are at their best when used in simple preparations as evidenced by butter braised beans with tomato and ale that arrive atop a thickly sliced piece of brioche and is further capped off by a fried egg. A limited dessert menu should not be missed. An indulgent sticky toffee pudding—a date-studded, sherry-infused affair—gets drizzled with caramel and cream and is absolutely heavenly.

Kris, Bella Vista, 1100 S. 11th St., Philadelphia, PA 19147; (215) 468-0104; krisphilly.com; Italian; $$$. Those who remember Chef-Owner Kristian Leuzzi's eponymously titled foray into fine dining still dream about the food—and remember the heartbreak when he decided to shutter Kristian's. That heartbreak has now turned into critical acclaim for his new casual concept, appropriately titled Kris. Already gaining a legion of loyalists, the menu wows with simple preparations of grilled octopus and braised calamari in a light tomato broth. The casual concept is further reinforced with offerings like crispy and addictive polenta "fries," a lamb burger, and the deliciously briny caper-studded salmon "PLT" (the 'P' is for prosciutto). Among the heartier mains: venison osso buco and pork chop Milanese.

L'Angolo Ristorante Italiano, South Philadelphia; 1415 W. Porter St., Philadelphia, PA 19145; (215) 389-4252; salentorestaurant.com; Italian; $$. Most neighborhood residents would prefer if no one knew about this place—it is that good. In an area bursting with Italian options, to earn a reputation as the best in

the city is a testament to the menu's
quality. Although it may not be wise
to fill up prior to the main event,
the *funghi al forno*—rosemary-tinged
baked wild mushrooms swaddled in
a layer of creamy fontina—is a great
choice. Be prepared to be bowled over by

the airy homemade ricotta gnocchi in cream sauce or the heartier
Bolognese and keep a hopeful eye out for menu specials.

The Latest Dish, Queen Village; 613 S. 4th St., Philadelphia, PA
19147; (215) 629-0565; latestdish.com; New American; $$. This
appropriately named restaurant offers an eclectic menu featuring
a variety of cuisines—perfect for diners who can't make up their
minds. Duck rolls, seitan meat loaf, and crab and cheese wontons
are some of the signature dishes, but the mac and cheese remains
a tried-and-true favorite. Order a drink from the extensive beer or
wine lists, grab a seat at the bar, and snack on the lemongrass
mussels.

Le Virtù, Bella Vista/Southwark; 1927 E. Passyunk Ave.,
Philadelphia, PA 19148; (215) 271-5626; levirtu.com; Italian; $$$.
Since its inception, Le Virtù has shone as a beacon of authentic
Italian cuisine and, over the years, has progressed from traditional
Abruzzese fare to a more refined, modernized menu. Young execu-
tive chef Joe Cicala breathes new life in the South Philadelphia stal-
wart with a menu deferential to tradition but infused with a touch

of innovation. Locavores may note that much of the aged *salumi* is crafted using pigs from nearby Berks County farms. Divine antipasti like the porchetta-filled fried olives and baked polenta crowned with crispy guanciale set the stage for a host of notable *primi* and—if there's room—*secondi*. Impressive are the handkerchief pasta with a rich duck *ragù* and a braised lamb shank atop a saffron risotto. A fairly sweeping wine list presents selections according to Italian region though a glass of grappa is still an option. The dessert menu just may usher you into sensory overload with its offerings, but the fried chestnut- and chocolate-filled ravioli and anise-tinged Italian beignets may prove too delectable to resist.

Little Delicious, Angora; 4821 Woodland Ave., Philadelphia, PA 19143; (215) 729-4911; Caribbean/Jamaican; $. There is no shortage of ethnic food in Philadelphia, but many feel there is a shortage of authentic Jamaican cuisine. Little Delicious is one of those places that you'll miss if you blink, so keep your eyes peeled when tooling around the neighborhood of Angora or you'll miss out on the most amazing platters of curried goat with rice and peas and steamed cabbage—the sides are the perfect foil to meltingly tender goat that seems to fall off the bone with the slightest touch of the fork. Hailed as Jamaica's national dish, true diehards should try the ackee and salt-fish; Little D also hits it out of the park with the flavorful stewed chicken. Portions are large and filling, with a large order providing enough for two, so order accordingly. Cash only.

Los Gallos Mexican Taqueria, South Philadelphia; 951 Wolf St., Philadelphia, PA 19148; (215) 551-1245; losgallosphilly.com; Mexican; $. Area residents are pretty possessive about their beloved Los Gallos—harboring the kind of reluctance that comes with not wanting to share your best secret. It's understandable, but this place is too good to keep tucked away. Chef-Owner Luis Jimenez does the cooking and serving at this little bodega and churns out authentic *tortas,* tacos, and enchiladas that have created quite the buzz. Spicy, crumbly chorizo is heaped onto an open-faced double corn tortilla and topped with a generous pile of nopales. Pineapple-studded *al pastor* is a flavorful mash-up of savory spit-roasted pig tinged by the sweetness of the fruit; enchiladas are served stacked rather than rolled and offer alternating layers of tortillas, *queso fresco,* refried beans, and avocado with a choice of meat on the side. Tucking into inky black *huitlacoche*-stuffed quesadillas requires a bit of an adventurous spirit, but will reward your palate if you can get past the origin of the main ingredient. Even if you're the type who prefers Mexican food "dry" (sans salsa), don't skip the bowls of vivid salsa verde or the fresh corn salsa; there's also a decent offering of Mexican beverages. Since this place doubles as a grocery store as well, it's a good idea to purchase some authentic goods and imports to take home.

MUNCHING WITH MINI-FOODIES

Let's face it: most children are becoming more and more discerning when it comes to the food they eat. What did we expect? As adults, we have become more fascinated with the culinary world and our tastes certainly have changed within the past decade or so—even the way we view food has changed. Of course, what's good for the goose is good for the gander and now we have birthed a legion of mini-foodies. There's no denying that the city of Philadelphia is a food lover's paradise and that includes several dining options for the little ones. From dim sum to Italian classics, Philly's got your tiny tot covered.

Bridget Foy's, *Society Hill; 200 South St., Philadelphia, PA 19147; (215) 922-1813; bridgetfoys.com; Traditional American; $$.* Wisconsin cheddar–topped mini sliders, veggie flatbread and homemade spinach ravioli are standouts on the kids' menu, but don't discount options from the regular menu as well. Bridget's can get noisy on the weekend, which may be the perfect place to mask the din of rowdy (or temper tantrum prone) kiddies.

Dim Sum Garden, *Chinatown; 59 N. 11th St., Philadelphia, PA 19107; (215) 627-0218; Asian; $.* If you're looking for a fancy schmancy place, you'll be disappointed in this Chinatown hotspot, but those in the know will appreciate this place for what it is: an awesome dumpling house where your kids can slurp up some of the best dim sum in the city. See p. 75 for more information.

Famous 4th Street Delicatessen, *Queen Village; 700 S. 4th St., Philadelphia, PA 19147; (215) 922-3274; famous4thstreetdelicatessen .com; Deli; $$.* Be forewarned: Even though the sandwiches are offered in "regular" and "zaftig" varieties, both options are probably taller than your child. Reminiscent of a New York Jewish deli, hot roast beef, pastrami, and corned beef are among the most popular options; but if your little one isn't meshugganah for these classic deli treats, there's always the chicken or egg salad. For a sweet ending, treat the kiddies to a black-and-white cookie. See p. 126 for more information.

The Franklin Fountain, *Old City; 116 Market St., Philadelphia, PA 19106; (215) 627-1899; franklinfountain.com; Ice Cream Shop; $.* There's not a single menu item that you'll have to convince your child to eat. Why? Because it's all about ice cream here! You'll get a kick out of the retro, old-timey vibe and decor and who can resist sharing a gargantuan ice cream sundae topped with hot fudge that's made in-house? See p. 40 for more information.

Jones, *Market East, 700 Chestnut St., Philadelphia, PA 19106; (215) 238-9600; jones-restaurant.com; New American; $$.* Famed restaurateur Stephen Starr pays homage to the era of shag carpet and disco with this Brady Bunch–esque eatery. It's kitschy and cool and your budding foodie can enjoy baked mac and cheese, pistachio-crusted tilapia, or if you've got a baby beefeater, the brisket.

Morning Glory Diner, *Bella Vista; 735 S. 10th St., Philadelphia, PA 19147; (215) 413-3999; themorningglorydiner.com; Traditional American/Diner; $$.* This is the place to go when your kid wakes you up extra early on the weekends. Heed the insistence of your pint-sized insomniac to get up and get dressed and head to the diner for some waffles and eggs. See p. 139 for more information.

SquareBurger, *Franklin Square; 200 N. 6th St., Philadelphia, PA 19106; historicphiladelphia.org/franklin-square; Traditional American; $.* Franklin Square, one of Philadelphia's five public squares, is literally a kids' playground—complete with a carousel, miniature golf course, and Stephen Starr's burger shack. When hunger strikes, grab your little one a juicy burger on a Martin's potato roll and an order of classic crinkle-cut fries.

Moe's Hot Dog House, Grays Ferry; 2601 Washington Ave., Philadelphia, PA 19146; (215) 465-6637; moeshotdoghouse.com; Hot Dogs/Traditional American; $. Finding Moe's takes a bit of effort—it's nestled away in the middle of a warehouse district and located near busy highways, but it's worth the trek to get your hands on one of Moe's dogs. Any hot dog lover would concede that toppings are great, but a truly good hot dog can stand on its own, and Moe's definitely understands this. Using famed Levis hot dogs, the offerings are pretty extensive and range from the Billy Penn (a plain hot dog named after the city's founder) and Connie

Mac (topped with mac and cheese) to the heat-inducing Engine #47, whose spiciness can be adjusted from 1 to 3 alarms. Moe's further endears itself to its customers by serving breakfast (don't miss the sweet potato pancakes) and a notable lunch roster of sandwiches and hoagies with a fish cake thrown in for good measure.

Monsu, Italian Market; 901 Christian St., Philadelphia, PA 19147; (215) 440-0495; monsurestaurant.com; Italian; $$. At this tiny Italian Market BYOB, Chef-Owner Peter McAndrews of **Paesano's** fame (p. 46) takes *arancini* and turns them on their head. Actually, he flattens the traditionally spherical risotto ball and stuffs it with a tender short rib *ragù* instead of the typical Parma ham. The result is a crispy crust with a creamy center that will make you swoon, but know that this type of reaction is pretty much standard when tasting anything McAndrews makes. He is one of a handful of chefs who, through frequent travels abroad, have brought rustic Italian cooking and techniques back to the Italian Market section of the city. A dish of light and airy ricotta gnocchi with crab is a revelation as is the *scamorza*—a grilled smoked mozzarella with watercress and prickly pear puree.

Morning Glory Diner, Bella Vista; 735 S. 10th St., Philadelphia, PA 19147; (215) 413-3999; themorningglorydiner .com; Traditional American/Diner; $$. Even before the popularity of TV shows devoted to showcasing diners, Philadelphia has long been a city that loves its diners. As is typical of most diners, a Morning Glory breakfast like challah french toast or the focaccia breakfast sandwich is a great way to jump-start your day but don't discount its lunchtime fare because the fresh homemade soups and macaroni and five cheeses rival Mom's. Weekend brunch is a pretty impressive affair and worth rising early to beat the gathering crowd.

Nam Phuong, Bella Vista; 1100 Washington Ave., Philadelphia, PA 19147; (215) 468-0410; namphuongphilly.com; Vietnamese; $. Inexpensive (and huge) bowls of pho make this a prime destination for the hungry and frugal alike. There are several different types of meat that can accompany your pho choice; the tender chicken-flecked pho, in a rich chicken broth whose surface is dotted with cilantro and thinly sliced onions, is so warm and welcoming as the noodles are left to rest at the bottom and soak up all the deliciousness of the broth. Accoutrements in the form of bean sprouts and lime are provided on the side. Even though pho is the obvious star, there are other menu highlights as well. Pliant grape leaves get stuffed with seasoned and grilled ground beef and are served with vermicelli. The Vietnamese spring rolls vary a bit from their Chinese counterparts—thinner and bolstered by a vinegary dipping sauce. It may be a smart choice to bring a group of friends to join in the noshing as portions can be overwhelming.

Nick's Charcoal Pit, South Philadelphia; 1242 Snyder Ave., Philadelphia, PA 19148; (215) 271-3750; Barbecue/Sandwiches; $. A bit of a dive, the place is a cramped storefront whose staff doesn't waste time exchanging pleasantries, but it's a great place for barbecue lovers to indulge in some finger-licking dry-rubbed ribs and grilled (or broiled) wings. For city dwellers short on outdoor grilling space, Nick's is an oasis in the desert. In addition to flame-grilled barbecue, there's an impressive turn of sandwiches that get a boost from **Sarcone's** rolls (p. 158)—the tender filet mignon sandwich with spinach and sharp provolone may just lure stalwart fans of the cheesesteak away from the hyped sandwich. It tends to get busy here so call ahead so you can grab your grub and go.

Nick's Old Original Roast Beef, South Philadelphia; 2149 S. 20th St., Philadelphia, PA 19145; (215) 463-4114; nicksroastbeef

.com; Traditional American/Sandwiches; $. Nick's is an old dive bar that not only exudes that old school South Philly charm but happens to serve what many consider to be a superior roast beef sandwich. While Nick's offers a limited variety of respectable sandwiches, why anyone would want to order anything other than juicy roast beef on a kaiser roll is baffling. After all, the roast beef is famous and deservedly so; it's pretty hard to resist the perfectly rare meat. This is a place that loves its au jus; sandwiches can even be ordered "extra wet." To complete the experience, be sure to order your sandwich with sharp provolone and grab a side of the famed gravy fries— thick-cut fries topped with tender chunks of roast beef and soaked in pan drippings.

Nomad Pizza, Bella Vista; 611 S. 7th St., Philadelphia, PA 19147; (215) 238-0900; nomadpizzaco.com; Italian/Pizza; $$. There's good news for Philly pizza lovers—it's no longer necessary to trek to New Jersey or rent their super-tricked out REO Speedwagon to snag a pie from Nomad Pizza. Owners Tom Grim and Stalin Bedon have opened an additional physical location in the city. The bi-level pizzeria features a cozy downstairs with a couple of communal tables where you can catch a glimpse of all the pie-making magic and a full bar and larger eating area upstairs (complete with a movie projector and screen). An exact replica of the oven found in the mobile wagon, it's hard not to be mesmerized by the copper-domed beauty whose maximum temperature reaches a fiery 850° which perfectly blisters the Neapolitan style pizzas from raw to cooked in an unbelievable

90 seconds. The pies are crafted from locally sourced, all-organic products whenever possible and the result is a delicious, succinct menu of about 12 pizzas and a handful of artfully done salads. While there are no real misses on the menu, the tartufo, spicy sausage, and margherita pies are obvious winners.

Penrose Diner, South Philadelphia; 2016 Penrose Ave., Philadelphia, PA 19145; (215) 465-1097; penrosediner.com; Traditional American/Diner; $. Being served a piece of pie and a cup of coffee at the counter by a waitress who calls you "hun" or scarfing down some waffles and a "coupla" eggs while nursing a hangover—this is what a classic diner is all about and that's exactly what you'll get at Penrose. Happily, this is an old-school neighborhood staple where pancakes are not called galettes and bacon isn't referred to as *lardons*. Cheap eats, daily specials, and a variety of sandwiches; it's familiar, unfussy comfort food at its best.

Pete's Pizza, Southwest Philadelphia; 7229 Passyunk Ave., Philadelphia, PA 19142; (215) 365-3775; Italian/Pizza; $. Not much to look at and offering no seating, Pete's is one of those in-and-out joints that fly under the radar—quietly serving some of the city's best cheesesteaks, pizzas, and wings while the more recognizable names garner the attention, but that's OK. Neighborhood residents, who have been frequenting Pete's for years, are more than willing to keep this place a secret. The inexpensive menu makes it an ideal place to grab a stromboli, fries, or a little something extra to munch on on those tailgating days.

Pho Saigon, Pennsport; 1100 S. Columbus Blvd., Philadelphia, PA 19147; (267) 773-7305; Vietnamese; $. In the city, pho can be a hit or miss endeavor, but the piping hot bowls of meat-laden  Vietnamese rice noodles at this strip-mall eatery are delicious. The menu is pretty extensive and diverse and offers a number of noodle and broken rice dishes, vermicelli, *bo kho,* and appetizers. Start off with must-try spring rolls before progressing to the main dish. The fresh fruit juice bar is a nice added touch; try an unusual avocado smoothie or the salty lemon.

Pub on Passyunk East, South Philadelphia; 1501 E. Passyunk Ave., Philadelphia, PA 19147; (215) 755-5125; pubonpassyunkeast .com; Traditional American; $$. You've got to appreciate a city that lavishes praise on dive bars like The P.O.P.E (as it's commonly called). Nestled deep in the heart of a South Philly neighborhood, this pub is as well known for its beer list as it is for its outstanding menu. POPE doesn't shy away from pub grub—in fact, the classics are embraced here and given a little nudge. Expect to find the usual suspects like chicken wings, nachos, and burgers but be pleasantly surprised when those wings are glazed with a habañero molé, vegans are given the option to top their nachos with seasoned seitan, and vegetarians can opt for the homemade kasha burger. It's nice to know there's a place for everyone at the bar.

Salt & Pepper, Bella Vista; 1623 E. Passyunk Ave., Philadelphia, PA 19148; (215) 238-1920; saltandpepperphilly.com; New American; $$$. This quaint little BYOB (only on Tues and Wed) recently packed up and moved from its Queen Village digs and entered the big leagues. That is, it opened up shop on hot, up-and-coming East Passyunk Avenue—the "it" avenue that several hipster shops and notable restaurants call home. The menu offers highlights like an unusual pineapple and beet salad, which normally make strange bedfellows, but totally work in this dish. A dark, rich French onion soup gets a global infusion with the addition of kalamata olives, mascarpone, and Parmesan cheese and the result is a cheesy, slightly briny delight. Noteworthy mains like the orecchiette tossed with lobster and the rack of lamb with eggplant "caviar" should not be missed; honorable mention for the more casual burgers. If you don't care to BYO, there is a limited wine list.

Santucci's Original Square Pizza, Bella Vista; 901 S. 10th St., Philadelphia, PA 19147; (215) 825-5304; santuccispizza.com; Italian/Pizza; $$. In South Philadelphia, how does a pizzeria distinguish itself from the pizza-slinging masses? One way is to simply change the shape of your pies—as evidenced by Santucci's, whose square pies have become the stuff of legends. The shape isn't the only thing that's unique about the pizza—the construction itself is unusual. Freshly made dough is topped with sliced whole-milk mozzarella then gets generously slathered with a sweet tomato sauce; by laying down the "protective" layer of cheese the pizza is saved from sogginess. Starters, sides, and salads (consider the antipasto board), sandwiches and burgers, and the signature meatballs (a beef, veal, and wild boar blend) fill out the menu. This is not your typical casual restaurant—most of the menu consists of ingredients made in-house like the hand-cut sweet and white potato fries and the house-cured pancetta; even the desserts are made on the premises. Much to the delight of Center City and South Philly residents, this location now delivers.

Scannicchio's, South Philadelphia; 2500 S. Broad St., Philadelphia, PA 19145; (215) 468-3900; scannicchio.com; Italian; $$. With this location, city dwellers don't have to trek to the Atlantic City original. While the tight quarters may be a deterrent to the claustrophobic, most are willing to forgo elbow room to enjoy noteworthy starters like bruschetta, *ravioli fritti,* and whole stuffed artichokes. Choose a dish or two from the list of varied antipasti before delving into more substantial plates of manicotti, gnocchi, or spicy fra diavolo. Normally reserved for the holiday season in many traditional Italian establishments, the special "seven fish" dinner—consisting of an array of *pesce* served over linguine—is offered as part of the regular menu.

Sidecar Bar & Grille, Graduate Hospital; 2201 Christian St., Philadelphia, PA 19146; (215) 732-3429; thesidecarbar.com; New American/Gastropub; $$. Though it looks a bit forlorn on the corner of Christian Street, Sidecar may quite possibly be the ideal gastropub where classics like wings and nachos get tasty makeovers but are even further outdone by tender Carolina pulled pork, steamed Prince Edward Island mussels in a tomato broth, and shrimp and grits. The burgers here enjoy a pretty high ranking in the city and deservedly so; a gruyère-topped burger with truffled mayo crowned with a crispy egg is one of the many must-order items. Even the fries, so often subjected to being second-fiddle players to the main attraction, are worth ordering. A meticulously crafted beer list presents a host of choices for hops junkies, including gluten-free options, and rotates regularly. Weekend brunch can be a crowded affair—especially in the tight quarters of the first floor—but head upstairs to the recently opened space to enjoy eye openers like crab Benedict or chorizo gravy and buttermilk biscuits.

Southwark, Queen Village; 701 S. 4th St., Philadelphia, PA 19147; (215) 238-1888; southwarkrestaurant.com; New American; $$$. There's no denying it—Southwark's beautiful dark wood interior and long bar up the sexiness quotient exponentially. Husband-and-wife owners Sheri and Kip Waide's French-inflected fare has garnered a band of loyalists who delight in a menu crafted from locally sourced, heirloom, and heritage ingredients. A warm Shellbark Farms parmesan and herb-crusted goat cheese with poached apple and honey,

steamed clams swathed in a dried chile broth and spicy fried quail are favorites. An extensive cocktail menu is a mixology aficionado's dream, with sips like the Hanky Panky—a gin and sweet vermouth concoction with a dash of the famed Italian bitter Fernet-Branca—and an authentic Hemingway daiquiri. Along with the hefty offering of cocktails, draft and bottled beers and wine prove complementary to any meal. In the warmer months, take advantage of the bistro-like outdoor seating and you'll believe you've been transported to another continent.

Taqueria la Veracruzana, Bella Vista; 908 Washington Ave., Philadelphia, PA 19147; (215) 465-1440; Mexican; $. Immigration has helped to change the landscape of the Italian Market and, thankfully, that means the presence of a number of Mexican, Vietnamese, and Thai restaurants dotted among the long-established Italian eateries that gave the area its name. The taqueria is definitely no-frills, so if you're a stickler for presentation and white tablecloths, you should probably dine elsewhere. Highly recommended are the platters of flavorful, well-seasoned *al pastor,* colossal burritos, and authentic tacos—you won't find your typical drive-thru impostors here. A selection of mild and spicy house-made salsas adds a fresh kick to the meal, but if you find that too tame, opt for the oddly pleasing jalapeño taco—a cheese-stuffed pepper housed squarely in a corn tortilla. There are often specials offered on the weekends; keep an eye out for these tasty whims.

Terryin Restaurant and Bar, Pennsport; 358 Snyder Ave., Philadelphia, PA 19148; (215) 218-2888; Sushi/Asian Fusion; $. There are a number of upscale, pricey sushi restaurants in the city that command top dollar, but it's really the unsuspecting, hidden spots that are the real deal. From the outside, this South Philly hole-in-the-wall doesn't look like much, but sushi seekers in the know realize just how special this place really is. Admittedly, Terryin has a bit of an identity crisis—there's a smidgen of Japanese/Chinese fusion going on and the menu offers a hybrid mix of fare. Sushi chefs create specialties like the dynamite roll (tempura-fried crab, salmon, and asparagus) and California roll at lightning speeds with such precision it makes you feel like you're being treated to a live performance. If you're squeamish about raw sushi, the cooked options are just as delicious. Terryin also does a fine job of non-sushi Chinese standards like General Tso's chicken and pork dumplings. Those seeking authentic libations will appreciate the decent selection of sake and Japanese beer.

Post-Midnight Munching

Cantina Los Caballitos, Bella Vista; 1651 E. Passyunk Ave., Philadelphia, PA 19148; (215) 755-3550; cantinaloscaballitos.com; Mexican/Late Night; $$. Mexican food is often synonymous with late-night noshing. Although not backed by any scientific research, there may actually be a part of the brain programmed to crave anything stuffed in a shell or wrapped in a flour tortilla after midnight. There's something so right about scarfing down a carnitas taco loaded with guac and cheese or tucking into a platter of fried plaintains and washing it down with an insanely delicious blood orange margarita. A hybrid mix of bar and restaurant, this neighborhood spot enjoys a diverse and funky crowd—even enticing residents from distant parts of the city to mix and mingle with the locals. Bring a group of friends (or make new ones at the bar) and try some of the tequila flights. At 1 a.m., you're probably not interested in learning the subtle differences between *reposado* and *añejo,* but sampling quality tequilas in a friendly neighborhood bar is probably the most fun and entertaining "education" you'll ever receive.

Royal Tavern, Bella Vista; 937 E. Passyunk Ave., Philadelphia, PA 19147; (215) 389-6694; royaltavern.com; New American/Late Night; $$. Considered one of the restaurants that helped to usher in Philadelphia's gastropub era, Royal Tavern may sit unsuspectingly on Passyunk Avenue but once inside, you'll appreciate the jukebox-filled air and a menu of classics with elevated pub-grub flair. A vegan sloppy joe and a grilled sweet potato *bánh mì* reside on the menu just as comfortably as an Angus burger with caramelized onions, smoked Gouda, and pickled long hots and a comforting grilled cheese sandwich. Pull up a seat at the bar and you'll find yourself wondering when chicken wings got sexy. Here, they come in not only the traditional buffalo style but also glazed with a chipotle barbecue or a mango habañero sauce and are accompanied by pickled daikon and carrots and a tangy Gorgonzola ranch dressing—stick with one style or go for the gusto and sample all three. A jukebox that houses an eclectic mix of music, kicked-up comfort food, and a bar that offers something for everyone: a winning trifecta in anyone's book.

S & H Kebab House, Queen Village; 611 E. Passyunk Ave., Philadelphia, PA 19147; (267) 639-3214; kebabhouseonline.com; Middle Eastern/Late Night; $$. A kebab house that stays open until 3 a.m. (on Fri and Sat) sounds like the answer to a late night diner's prayers. Dining here is what you would imagine a Turkish birthday party to be—a fun- and food-filled affair complete with plenty of belly dancing. Going beyond standards like falafel, hummus, and baba ghanoush, the comprehensive menu offers just about every delicacy in the Middle Eastern repertoire. Of course the kebabs here, made with local and organic ingredients, are standouts—lamb, chicken, and Turkish meatball varieties are not to be missed. A handful of *soteler* (sautées and casseroles) dishes like *etli guvec* (a vegetable-studded lamb casserole), and *manti* (lamb-stuffed dumplings) allow you to delve deeper into the cuisine. Like most Middle Eastern confections, desserts like baklava tend to be a tad sugary but redemption arrives in the form of the lighter, oven-baked rice pudding that offers just the slightest hint of vanilla.

Tony Luke's, South Philadelphia; 39 E. Oregon Ave., Philadelphia, PA 19148; (215) 551-5725; tonylukes.com; Traditional American/Late Night; $. Situated next to an underpass in a less-than-exciting section of the city, there stands a beacon of sandwich artistry—the famed Tony Luke's. Many a midnight muncher has found himself craving a hit-the-spot sandwich from this legendary hotspot. Owner Tony Luke Jr. recently dropped nearly 100 pounds from his once-hulking frame—no thanks to his artery-clogging menu, which offers a nearly endless roster of authentic Philly sandwiches. Of course, a menu claiming to tout real-deal eats must include the famous cheesesteak and certainly Tony Luke's ranks among the best in the city, but don't miss out on what many Philadelphians consider the real Philly sandwich: Italian roast pork. Stuffed in a soft and appropriately chewy roll, spicy pork that has been marinated in a rich jus is piled high with garlicky broccoli rabe and sharp provolone. Indecisiveness may ensue when you consider additional offerings like the chicken cutlet parmesan, sausage and peppers, or the "beef buster" (roast beef with special sauce and bacon) sandwich.

Specialty Stores, Markets & Producers

Artisan Boulanger Patissier, Bella Vista; 1648 S. 12th St., Philadelphia, PA 19148; (215) 271-4688; artisanboulangerpatissier .com; French/Bakery; $. Turn a corner in South Philadelphia and you're likely to happen upon an Italian bakery—they are everywhere. To find an authentic Parisian bakery is a treat indeed; fresh-baked artisanal breads, pastries, and a host of confections make up the menu. The *pain au chocolat,* with a rich ribbon of chocolate tucked inside, is divine as are the almond and pistachio croissants. The wares are a tad pricier than those offered elsewhere, but a trip here is well worth the extra coin.

Cacia Bakery, South Philadelphia; 1526 W. Ritner St., Philadelphia, PA 19145; (215) 334-1340; caciabakery.com; Italian/Bakery; $. As one of the last few bakeries that still employ a brick oven, Cacia has churned out consistently delicious pizzas, stromboli, breads, and desserts for years and has even opened additional locations in Pennsylvania and nearby New Jersey. The neighborhood staple became famous for its Pizzazz—a white American cheese pie topped with a variety of hot peppers—which is a must when visiting the area. For the budding sandwich maker, the individual rolls and breads are ideal for crafting hoagies and cheesesteaks at home or, if you dare, attempting to recreate Cacia's roast pork sandwich. Weekends are extremely busy and the line usually snakes out the door, so placing an order ahead of time is wise.

Cannuli House of Pork, Italian Market; 937 S. 9th St., Philadelphia, PA 19147; (215) 922-2988; Butcher Shop; $. You've got to appreciate a place that calls itself a house of pork—it doesn't get any better than that. The cast of characters that make up the staff are part of this butcher shop's charm; not only do they offer to season your meat but they'll also send you home with a bone or two for Fido if you ask. Cannuli's also does an impressive turn of various cuts of meats—lamb chops, pork shoulder, and the like—but for most who make the trip to the Italian Market, it's all about the sausage. Hot Italian sausage and perhaps the best chorizo in the area are definite buys but don't let that discourage you from selecting a slab of their bacon as well.

Claudio's Specialty Foods, Italian Market; 924-26 S. 9th St., Philadelphia, PA 19147; (215) 627-1873; claudiofood.com; Specialty/Gourmet; $$. Olive oils, tapenades, vinegars, pastas, and a bevy of imported goods grace the shelves at Claudio's, where engaging in a conversation with the knowledgeable staff about whether to purchase Locatelli or Parmesan is likely to yield a wealth of information about provenance, subtleties in taste, and the merits of both. Here, they know their stuff and are thankfully willing to share. In the tiny (and often crowded) shop, *salumi* and cheese hang from the ceiling and long cases of specialty meats and cheeses are on display; shoebox-like cases and barrels offer smaller delectables near the front of the store. For a true (and somewhat frantic) Italian Market experience, visit during the holidays when droves of shoppers descend upon the diminutive Claudio's and fill it to the rafters.

Dad's Stuffings, Bella Vista; 1615 W. Ritner St., Philadelphia, PA 19145; (215) 334-1934; Meat Shop/ Caterer; $. Many an unworthy home cook has been the recipient of praise for turning out beautiful dinners when, in reality, all they did was take a trip to Dad's to stock up on hearty and filling prepared foods and a few side dishes to pass off as their own. Local pastas come in fresh and frozen varieties, prepared salads are delicious, and the homemade sauces are perfectly seasoned, but what (obviously) put Dad's on the map is the variety of stuffings it sells that can also be tucked into chicken breasts at your request. If you want to avoid the cacophony and teeming crowds of the Italian Market but still want quality fare and the old-school feel, Dad's is a safe (and wise) bet.

Di Bruno Brothers, Italian Market; 930 S. 9th St., Philadelphia, PA 19147; (215) 922-2876; dibruno.com; Specialty/Gourmet; $$. As it is popular among the more affluent set, be prepared to part with some serious cash if you're planning on sampling the best of what this specialty store has to offer. Di Bruno has earned a reputation as being the go-to place for high-end gourmet rarities and, judging from the shelves stocked with *pâte de fruits*, mustards from Burgundy, and an array of foreign imports, it's easy to see that the reputation is well deserved. A line of private label grocery items are offered as well as cured meats, a comprehensive selection of obscure cheeses, and antipasti. The gregarious and helpful staff is always willing to offer insight and guidance in the selection process; consider yourself lucky should you be the recipient of some of this vast knowledge. If you're looking for something a little more formal, tastings can be arranged; call the store for booking information. Di Bruno Brothers has an additional store (and upstairs cafe) at 1730 Chestnut St., Philadelphia, PA 19103; (215) 665-9220; check the website for additional locations.

Esposito's Meats, Italian Market; 1001 S. 9th St., Philadelphia, PA 19147; (215) 922-2659; espositosmeats.com; Butcher Shop; $$. An impressive selection of meats and the staff's friendly "have-it-your-way" attitude are the hallmarks of this South Philly butcher shop. Here, meats are cut to customers' specifications with no whim too outrageous to satisfy. Ground meats, steaks, chicken and pork are all reasonably priced as is their decent selection of lobster tails, frozen shrimp, sausages, and cheeses. It can get busy and crowded on the weekends, but most days the staff is willing to chat and share cooking tips.

Green Aisle Grocery, Bella Vista; 1618 E. Passyunk Ave., Philadelphia, PA 19148; (215) 465-1411; greenaislegrocery.com; Specialty/Gourmet; $$$. A stroll through this specialty grocer is like visiting all of your favorite local restaurants in one location. Many area chefs sell their signature products here—pasta from New Jersey-based Severino, the divine hummus from **Zahav** (p. 101) and sausage from **Renaissance Sausage Truck** (p. 109) to name a few. The space itself is small and the selection of products is heavily dependent upon availability from local purveyors and farms, but this all adds to charm and the "specialness" of this South Philly charmer. Focused on offering the finest locally sourced products,

expect to find cheeses, yogurt, milk, meats, and produce from outlying farms. There's also a varied selection of honeys from local apiaries. As with most boutique grocers, shopping here can get pricey so don't plan on picking up your entire grocery list. The website offers updates on product availability, so if you have your heart set on a certain specialty item, it's a good idea to check first.

Hung Vuong Supermarket, Bella Vista; 1122 Washington Ave., Philadelphia, PA 19147; (215) 271-2505; Specialty Market/Grocery; $. Where to start? You could spend all day here sorting through the dizzying array of products at this catch-all supermarket. This is not necessarily the place to visit if you're not familiar with the cuisine—this is definitely a specialty market. You'll find everything from rows and rows of canned goods (think canned quail eggs), dry goods, and noodles to just about every kind of produce, meat, and seafood you can think of. Obscure imported candies, locally baked desserts, and a surprising offering of palm sugars cure those in need of a serious sweet fix. In the back of the store, there's a busy fish market that offers fresh-off-the-boat options and there's actually some still swimming. If you're in need of something to eat pronto, there's a tiny table near the produce section that offers near-perfect roast pork cleaved right from the bone while you wait. For more adventurous eaters, the menu offers a variety of pig parts and organ meat. Parking is a nightmare and can make for a frustrating visit (especially on the weekends and during weekday lunch hours), so your best bet is to visit during off-peak hours.

Ippolito's Seafood, Newbold; 1300 Dickinson St., Philadelphia, PA 19104; (215) 389-8906; ippolitoseafood.biz; Grocery/Seafood; $$. If you ever want to nurture your inner chef or shop like one, Ippolito's is the place to do it. Top local chefs know that its seafood market offers some of the freshest catches in the city, from live crabs (essential to crabs and spaghetti—a Philly favorite) to whole fish. For hard-to-find sea delicacies, make a phone call and it can

be ordered (season willing). The fishmongers here are always willing to discuss topics like source and sustainability with those who inquire. Cooked food can be ordered from the counter on the grocery side of the store where crab-stuffed mushrooms, seafood salads, and salmon burgers are so delicious, you'll almost forget you came here for the fresh seafood.

Isgro Pastries, Italian Market; 1009 Christian St., Philadelphia, PA 19147; (215) 923-3092; bestcannoli.com; Italian/Bakery; $$. You'll be hard-pressed to find a better cannoli in the city than at Isgro whose baking ovens have been churning out confections, pastries, and cookies for over 100 years. The display cases are always teeming with a host of goodies and, with Italian delicacies like *pignolata*, tiramisu, and *torrone* (a candy made with egg whites, candied fruits, and almonds), it's exactly what you think of when you envision an authentic, old-school neighborhood bakery. During the holidays (especially Christmas), it's best to call ahead and place your order—the bakery is sheer madness during the season.

Potito's Bakery, South Philadelphia; 1614 W. Ritner St., Philadelphia, PA 19145; (215) 334-2996; potitosbakery.com; Bakery; $$. Potito's is a classic Italian bakery and looks as if it could have easily been plucked from another era. The staff is friendly and always willing to offer an explanation should you not know the difference between *sfogliatelle* and cannoli. Serious sweet toothers will swoon over the various cannoli—ricotta, vanilla custard, chocolate, and mascarpone—and the addictive St. Joseph's cakes (zeppole). Potito's is no slouch in the bread department, either—before you're off on your sugar high, don't forget to pick up some freshly baked breads or even panettone. Many of the confections, especially the cannoli, tend to sell out early in the day so plan your trip accordingly.

Sarcone's Bakery, Italian Market; 758 S. 9th St., Philadelphia, PA 19147; (215) 922-0445; Italian/Bakery; $. People tend to wax poetic about this place—and rightfully so. In a city that loves anything between two slices of bread, everyone knows just what an important element bread is to the good sandwich equation. Ideally, it must be crusty on the outside while remaining soft on the inside. If you've enjoyed a great sandwich in the city, the likelihood that it was made with bread from Sarcone's is fairly high. The South Philadelphia bakery has been serving their brick-oven breads and rolls for over 80 years and, hands down, serves the best Italian bread in the entire city and is conveniently situated a few feet from its deli outpost. The tomato pie and pepperoni bread are popular choices; bread sells out at lightning speeds, so getting there early is mandatory. Sarcone's Deli has a suburban outpost as well at 230 W. Market St., West Chester, PA 19382.

Talluto's Authentic Italian Food, Italian Market; 944 S. 9th St., Philadelphia, PA 19147; (215) 627-4967; tallutos.com; Specialty Market/Grocery; $$. In the early 80s, retired chef Joe Talluto expanded his empire with a retail pasta facility and four Italian specialty markets as an offshoot to his wildly successful homemade ravioli shop. Today, Talluto's sits on the corner of 9th Street in the heart of the Italian Market and serves not only the fresh, homemade pasta that made it famous but also a number of specialties like beef tortellini, meatballs, and sauces. With a selection of olive oils, breads, fresh mozzarella, and the olive and antipasti bars, Talluto's is a one-stop shop.

Varallo Brothers Bakery, Bella Vista; 1639 S. 10th St., Philadelphia, PA 19148; (215) 952-0367; varallobrotherspastic ceria.com; Italian/Bakery; $. You could seriously exceed your day's caloric intake limit with a trip to Varallo's, but the traditional *zuccotto* (a semifrozen, brandy-infused cake and ice cream delight), *zuppa inglese* (trifle-like custard dessert), and the host of Italian cookies and pastries are worth every extra minute on the treadmill you may have to endure. Inexpensive loaves of crusty bread—perfect for sopping up gravy from your Sunday dinner plate—line the shelves as well. Cannoli wars are common in this part of town, with everyone claiming their favorite bakery makes the best; Varallo is definitely a contender and their storied cannoli are the stuff of which dreams are made.

West

University City, Walnut Hill, West Philadelphia

West Philadelphia is an area of the city known more for its universities than anything else. It owes its diverse dining field to throngs of East Asian, Latin American, West Indian, and African immigrants, but it owes its multitude of inexpensive dining options to the heavy cash-strapped student population. While the area's fine dining scene is a bit anemic, there are plenty of places of note that dot the landscape. Looking beyond some of greasy takeouts, diners will find in-your-face, unapologetic ethnic cuisine, healthy options, and innovative fare.

Landmark

Marigold Kitchen, University City; 501 S. 45th St., Philadelphia, PA 19104; (215) 222-3699; marigoldkitchenbyob.com; New American;

$$$. If this nearly 80-year-old BYOB had a more prestigious location—Center City perhaps—there would be a reservation waiting list a mile long. However, since it's doesn't, Marigold Kitchen is rarely overrun with diners, making for a lovely dining experience—and what an experience it is. An array of amuse-bouches pour out of the kitchen in a seemingly never-ending procession; some are delightful, some are not, but they're a nicely added touch nonetheless. Expect to find a menu of reworked classics with hints of newfangled molecular gastronomy (yes, there's foam). Innovative flourishes like the sweet raisin gel that accompanies the marinated *boquerones* or the texturally mixed heirloom beet salad can be shocking at first but the flavors are entirely recognizable once your palate has been initiated. The menu, focused on locally sourced ingredients, changes frequently but count on seafood, game, and duck to play starring roles.

Foodie Faves

Abyssinia, Walnut Hill; 229 S. 45th St., Philadelphia, PA 19104; (215) 387-2424; Ethiopian; $$. Ethiopian cuisine, cloaked in mystery, still remains unfamiliar to some. Residents in the know flock to this non-descript eatery for inexpensive, flavorful Ethiopian staples like *injera* (traditional flatbread) and *yebeg wot* (a stew made with tender morsels of lamb). Vegetarians and meat eaters alike can appreciate the piquant kick of slow-cooked spicy lentils known as *shiro wot* or *kik alicha* (a comforting yellow split pea stew). While Ethiopian cooking lends itself well to veggie dishes, unless you're a vegetarian, meat stews and a host of *yebeg* (lamb) and *siga* (beef) dishes are the way to go. If you want a true international experience, forgo the dining room and sidle up to the bar where Ethiopian nationals tend to gather to taste the foods of their homeland—a telling sign that Abyssinia is the real deal.

Aksum, Cedar Park; 4630 Baltimore Ave., Philadelphia, PA 19143; (267) 275-8195; aksumcafe.com; Mediterranean; $$. Oftentimes, Mediterranean restaurants fall prey to kitsch and overwhelm their spaces with knick knacks in an attempt to offer an authentic feel. Owner Saba Tedla doesn't rely on that kind of artifice at her recently opened spot—the space is coolly slick and exudes the kind of relaxed vibe that makes diners feel like they've been sucking on a hookah all day, which, by the way, is an experience offered at Aksum as well. Hearty soups, a variety of tapas, and large plates comprise the menu. Served cold, grape leaves are stuffed with a mix of savory herbs that vary slightly from more traditional varieties, and are an excellent choice as is the fried baby globe eggplant in a spiced arrabbiata sauce topped with fresh basil and ricotta salata. Progress to the *Aksumite tajin* (tagine)—a beautiful medley of slow-cooked eggplant, tomatoes, squash, and chickpeas ladled over Israeli couscous, or get carted away to Morocco with the slow braised lamb shanks that get a refreshing lift from a fresh coriander and parsley sauce. To finish, try the baklava laced with pomegranate-honey syrup.

Caribbean Cuisine, West Philadelphia; 6045 Baltimore Ave., Philadelphia, PA 19143; (215) 472-8553; Caribbean; $$. With all the restrictive bars on the windows, it's hard to tell if this place is really in business or if it was abandoned long ago. Rest assured, Caribbean Cuisine is open for business and dishing up huge platters of traditional Caribbean favorites. Toothsome but not too spicy curry chicken, oxtails, rice and beans, and cabbage are all good bets. There's a tiny seating area inside, but proves to be too cramped to really enjoy your meal in all its glory. It's best to grab and go somewhere worthwhile where you can properly chow down.

Dahlak, Cedar Park; 4708 Baltimore Ave., Philadelphia, PA 19143; (215) 726-6464; dahlakrestaurant.com; Eritrean/Ethiopian; $$. This West Philly restaurant/bar is often overshadowed by its Ethiopian neighborhood cousins, but it's no less noteworthy. Technically, the menu leans more toward Eritrean cuisine, which closely resembles that of neighboring Ethiopia (the differences are barely discernible). As is customary with this cuisine, food is served with *injera* (traditional spongy, slightly sour flatbread) and is communal and meant to be eaten by hand which makes for a relaxed (if not a little messy) dining experience. The meat dishes here are solid but, in terms of taste and preparation, it's really all about the vegetables. Impressively done lentils, collard greens with potatoes, and chickpeas are tasty, but if you're a spice seeker, the promise of even the spiciest dish can be disappointing as heat levels are sometimes a hit or miss. Surprisingly, beets make an appearance on the menu and offer an unexpected but welcome change to traditional notions of African cooking. If you're looking for libations, head to the bar in the back where inexpensive happy hour specials draw neighborhood crowds and interesting hot toddies are the perfect answer to a Philly winter. On warmer nights, head out back to a small patio area (which, admittedly, looks more like a cramped backyard than an outdoor bar space) for mingling and drinks.

Desi Chaat House, University City; 501 S. 42nd St., Philadelphia, PA 19104; (215) 386-1999; desichaathouse.com; Indian; $. Sticking out like a brightly colored sore thumb among the aged, rough-and-tumble landscape of West Philadelphia is this purveyor of Indian snack food, or *chaat* as it is more formally known. Indian snacks are unlike typical American snacks in that they're not junk food like potato chips or cheese curls but almost tapas-like in their appearance. Boiled potatoes, chickpeas, tempura-fried vegetables, and various chutneys are good examples of how what is considered humble in India can be a positively decadent snack to the uninitiated. The *Andhra chaat,* for example, is a savory blend of black-eyed peas, chickpeas, lentils, fresh curry leaves, and red chile. While it may be unfathomable that anything else other than *chaat* would be your meal of choice, Desi offers biryanis, soups, and wraps as well. If you experience a bit of spice overload and need a cooling down, try a traditional mango *lassi*—a yogurt-based fruit smoothie.

Distrito, University City; 3945 Chestnut St., Philadelphia, PA 19104; (215) 222-1657; distritorestaurant.com; Mexican; $$$. With loud, in-your-face colorful, and raucous Distrito, Chef José Garces offers Philadelphia elevated Mexican fare at a hefty price but it's worth every peso. Start with a boozy margarita and try not to fill up on chips and guacamole (good luck with that) before tasting the mushroom flatbread, carne Kobe and nopales tacos, or the District Chicken—a crisp-skinned wonder glazed with a chipotle-chile orange sauce served with addictively crunchy yucca fries. Various prix fixe tasting menus are available and offer a generous sampling of items not found on the regular menu. If your stomach (and wallet) allow, the churros are a must—just promise to not lick the plate.

Elena's Soul Lounge, Cedar Park; 4912 Baltimore Ave., Philadelphia, PA 19143; (215) 724-3043; elenassoul.com; Soul Food/Southern; $. Elena's is one of those hybrid places that just works; part music venue, part restaurant, and part bar, this tiny spot feeds the soul with music and food. Like most great places, Elena's itself is unassuming in a rather nondescript part of town, but crossing the threshold is like stepping into a magical era. The dining area exudes a funky '70s vibe (with a decor to match) that automatically lulls you into chill mode. There are no surprises on the menu—everything is straight out of the Soul Food 101 hand-book, but that's the beauty of Elena's. Its limited menu is a list of greatest hits of sorts—among them are what is deemed by some to be the best fried chicken in the city (take that, Mémé), smothered pork chops, and a roundup of down-home sides (the gooey mac and cheese shouldn't be missed). The mostly fried menu may not offer the healthiest fare; thankfully, heading upstairs to groove to live music and work off some calories is an option.

Green Line Cafe, Powelton Village; 3649 Lancaster Ave., Philadelphia, PA 19104; (215) 382-2143; greenlinecafe.com; Traditional American/Coffee & Tea; $. With three locations dotted around the city, this do-gooder mini-chain cafe has a feel-good ripple effect on its surrounding communities. Green Line serves fair-trade coffees, teas, and organic beverages; a light-fare menu of sandwiches and pastries is offered as well. Don't discount this coffeehouse as a one-trick pony, though. Touting a philosophy that encourages community involvement, the cafe hosts a number of art shows, live music happenings, and communal events.

Grill Fish Cafe, University City; 814 S. 47th St., Philadelphia, PA 19143; (215) 729-7011; Vietnamese; $$. As the name implies, Grill Fish is all about seafood. More specifically, the tight menu focuses on Vietnamese staples much like its big brother **Vietnam Cafe** (p. 172). The recently opened cafe is still tweaking its revolving menu but count on a whole grilled fish preparation nightly, like bass or branzino served on a bed of clear noodles. The sake-steamed mussels and clams and grilled octopus are simply prepared but are packed with subtle flavor. As the restaurant becomes more comfortable in its own skin, expect to see a more in-depth menu.

Honest Tom's Taco Shop, University City; 261 S. 44th St., Philadelphia, PA 19104; (215) 620-1851; Mexican; $. Lovers of Honest Tom's mobile food truck can now get their taco fix at this recently opened brick-and-mortar shop. "Honest" Tom McCusker first made noise on the streets of Philly with his tasty little tacos with big flavor profiles—people line up daily for sweet potato, plantain, chicken-and-pork, and the wildly popular fish tacos but by far the most sought-after menu item is the breakfast taco stuffed with scrambled eggs, crispy home fries, cheese, and fresh guacamole. Add some crumbled sausage and a healthy dose of hot sauce to jump start your morning. The menu changes often (as do operating hours), so be sure to call or follow the somewhat sporadic social media postings to find out the latest.

Kabobeesh, University City; 4201 Chestnut St., Philadelphia, PA 19104; (215) 386-8081; kabobeesh.com; Indian/Middle Eastern/ Halal; $. A carnivore's dream, the grill at this kebab house is a thing of beauty. Skewer upon skewer of seasoned chicken, lamb, and beef get the royal treatment and find themselves plated with warm rounds of naan, rice, and salad. Curries, tikka masala, and biryani may be standards but are prepared so thoughtfully that they end up being the ultimate comfort food. If you're feeling generous, try the *lahori chargha,* a large meal meant for sharing. A different special, including a vegetarian dish, is served daily so keep an eye out for the announcement board.

Kaffa Crossing, University City; 4423 Chestnut St., Philadelphia, PA 19104; (215) 386-0504; kaffacrossing.com; Ethiopian; $. Jaded West Philadelphians are used to the ethnic eateries that dot the landscape of their neighborhood, but even they realize what a gem Kaffa really is. It's a restaurant, hangout, and a stellar coffeehouse rolled into one. Heavy on veggie dishes, this place is a favorite haunt of nonmeat eaters. The slightly sour, spongy *injera* (a traditional Ethiopian bread) plays a starring role in many of the dishes like the bread salad *timatim fitfit*—a spiced panzanella-like mixture of tomatoes, onions, jalapeño, olive oil, and lemon juice. The rest of the menu offers North African classics like lentils, stews, and meat dishes that are tinged with cardamom, chile powder and *mitmita* (one of the staple regional spices).

Lee's Deli, Cedar Park; 4700 Baltimore Ave., Philadelphia, PA 19143; (215) 724-1954; Delis/Sandwiches; $. The very definition of a greasy spoon, Lee's captures the essence of all that a deli should be. It's another one of those places that neighborhood residents guard heavily, lest their beloved deli end up on the radar of tourists. The menu has a ton of specials, breakfast options, and sandwiches, which make it the perfect place to grab food any time of the day. Breakfast includes grab-and-go sandwiches and real-deal heartier fare like grits and eggs. Lunch is the big draw here and the fact that Lee's turns out what many consider the best cheesesteaks in the city is largely a neighborhood secret. It may be sacrilege to hardcore cheesesteak purists, but the chicken, broccoli, and provolone chicken cheesesteak is a must-try. Oh, and don't forget the desserts. Anyone who has ever wandered around the city trying to find the infamously elusive sweets vendor known only as "Cupcake Man" will be delighted to know that Lee's is one of the few re-sellers of his addictive carrot cake cupcakes.

Mood Cafe, University City; 4618 Baltimore Ave., Philadelphia, PA 19143; (215) 222-1037; moodcafephilly.com; Indian; $. Owner Hassan Bukhari, who coincidentally owns the local Desi Village and Desi Chaat House mini-chains, decided to do something a little different with his recently opened cafe. It's a coffeehouse hangout whose inexpensive menu is composed largely of international coffees and espresso, milkshakes, *lassis,*  shaved ice, and freshly squeezed fruit juices. A host of interesting and unusual syrups like rose and sandal-wood are used to flavor the shaved ice; figs, date, and mint are just a few choice mix-ins used for the thick shakes. Vegans needn't worry as there are almond, coconut, and soy milk options as well. While the beverages are top notch, Bukhari doesn't completely abandon his Indian roots; a menu of *chaat* and traditional dishes like *dhal* and *saag paneer* is available as well.

Nan Restaurant, University City; 4000 Chestnut St., Philadelphia, PA 19104; (215) 382-0818; nanrestaurant.com; French/Thai; $$$. Long before the term "fusion" crept into our lexicon, Nan Restaurant was blending French and Thai ingredients and techniques; the result is a menu where chicken curry resides alongside escargots. Expect to find thoughtfully done appetizers, artful salads, and mains. The Peking duck and pad thai are standouts; the crab spaghettini is also of note and is comforting in a way that only noodle slurping dishes can be. Desserts are made in-house; try the bread pudding or lemon tart. Service can be a little hit-or-miss but when it's good, it's great—don't let it discourage you from sampling some of the best food in the area.

Picnic, University City; 3131 Walnut St., Philadelphia, PA 19104; (215) 222-1608; picniceats.com; New American; $$. With its breath-of-fresh-air menu, Picnic fills a void in the West Philadelphia dining scene. The concept is cute and simple, the food is of the grab-and-go variety and perfect for—yes—outdoor picnics (although there is limited indoor seating). If you're sold on the idea of having an authentic picnic, there are even baskets for sale. The made-to-order menu boasts all-organic, fresh fare; sandwiches, salads, daily specials, and baked goods prove to be a great (and healthier) alternative to traditional takeout. Items are priced individually so building your own meal is an option and a great way to sample several different items. While the menu rotates often, favorites like the Dijon-tarragon chicken salad and the tuna niçoise salad remain a constant. The quinoa and chickpea salad and the Moroccan-inspired cumin/garlic/ paprika eggplant salad can stand alone as

mains or serve as side dishes. If available, try the Mexican chicken lasagna made with corn tortillas.

Saad's Halal Place, University City; 4500 Walnut St., Philadelphia, PA 19139; (215) 222-7223; saadhalal.com; Middle Eastern/Halal; $. Philadelphia is a city that loves its ethnic food—after all, this is the city where people argue over which street vendor sells the best falafel. While they're busy arguing over the food trucks, real food hunters know a little secret: Saad's may be the best place in the city to get falafel. Of course, this West Philly haunt does more than falafel well. The menu serves as a primer to Middle Eastern food with a few twists; baba ghanoush and hummus are plucked from their usual roles as dips for pita and reworked into sandwich form. The menu also takes a detour to Greece with classics like spinach pie and stuffed grape leaves; the grape leaf sandwich is a notable choice as well. Saad's also has an Americanized menu as well, but why anyone would want to venture to this neighborhood hotspot for anything other than shawarma, shish kebabs, and falafel is baffling.

Vientiane Cafe, University City; 4728 Baltimore Ave., Philadelphia, PA 19143; (215) 726-1095; Thai; $$. This bright, colorful storefront eatery is situated along the international strip of Baltimore Avenue and specializes in authentic Lao and Thai cuisine. The menu features curries, noodle dishes, spring rolls, soups, and pad thai. Try the steamed pork or chicken dumplings or the sweet coconut soup before moving to the *pad kee mao* (drunken noodles), which is billed as spicy but doesn't really move the heat dial. If you're seeking heat, be sure to ask for it extra spicy; mango or pineapple sticky rice complements the dishes well. To end the meal with a flourish, order the coconut ice cream, which arrives as a huge mound in a fresh half coconut. Cash only.

Vietnam Cafe, University City; 816 S. 47th St., Philadelphia, PA 19143; (215) 729-0260; eatatvietnam.com; Vietnamese; $$. Moving from its original smaller storefront next door was the right move for Vietnam Cafe. The new digs are bigger and flashier than the previous location and make diners feel like they're dining in an airy villa rather than West Philadelphia. Of course, there's more to this place than updated decor—the menu is fresh, authentic Vietnamese fare. Here, appetizers are amazing little bites that ready your palate for the pleasant onslaught of flavors to come. A crispy crepe-like pancake known as *banh xeo* is a shrimp- and pork-filled delight texturally offset with sweet onions and crunchy bean sprouts. In a dish of *thit nuong cuon,* char-grilled pork is enveloped in a delicate wrapping of rice paper and topped off with a chiffonade of basil. The rest of the menu is made up of rice dishes, rice vermicelli noodles, crispy noodles, soups, and heartier entrees. For a pleasantly citrusy kick, try the Vietnamese lemonade; if sweet endings are your thing, go for a scoop of the unusual red bean ice cream.

Wah-Gi-Wah, University City; 4447 Chestnut St., Philadelphia, PA 19104; (215) 921-5597; wah-gi-wah-halal.com; Pakistani/Halal; $.

Wah-gi-wah, "spectacular" in Punjabi, most certainly refers to this Pakistani eatery's most popular dish: fried chicken. Forget some of the better-known chicken joints in town; those with a serious poultry addiction know that some of the best fried bird is served here, although calling it fried chicken is oversimplifying matters a bit. Not only is it called by a different name—*lahori chargha*—it's seasoned with an unusual blend of spices mixed with yogurt and lime and slathered on a whole butterflied chicken before being fried. The result is chicken whose crust is more batter-like than the familiar crispy skin to which most diners are accustomed. Deeply rich curries, *karahi,* a hefty tandoori selection, and freshly baked bread round out the menu. Cool down a spicy tongue with a mango *lassi,* an old faithful favorite. If you're adventurous and like your drinks savory, sip on a salty *lassi*—definitely an acquired taste.

 ## Post-Midnight Munching

Fiume, Walnut Hill; 229 S. 45th St., Philadelphia, PA 19104; Late Night; $. Most people who know about this dive bar only received notice of its existence through the kind of word of mouth that usually indicates a cool hangout. Located above Ethiopian restaurant **Abyssinia** (p. 161) and accessible through the downstairs restaurant or an unmarked door on the side of the building, Fiume may be the hottest secret bar in West Philly. On any given night, the minuscule place is packed to the rafters. The dark ambience and privacy attract the university crowd; the bar boasts an awesome selection of bottled beers and the cocktails are amazing. Although not formally associated, the restaurant downstairs will sometimes serve food to the upstairs crowd, which helps stave off drunkenness for those who can't tolerate alcohol on an empty stomach. This is a great place to hang with a group of friends and impress them with the fact you actually know about this place. With musicians playing everything from Johnny Cash to bluegrass, you won't mind being packed like sardines with hippies, students, artists, and musicians. Cash only.

Makkah Market, University City; 4249 Walnut St., Philadelphia, PA 19104; (215) 382-0909; Middle Eastern/Late Night; $. Insomniacs and third-shift workers alike appreciate this 24/7 convenience store–like mecca of all things Middle Eastern. Inexpensive spices, harissa, grape leaves, hummus, an impressive assortment of groceries, and an on-site official halal butcher are the hallmarks of Makkah Market. Imported candies and snacks are fun to try for the adventurous and fresh tropical juices make for great late-night thirst quenchers. If round-the-clock grocery shopping doesn't appeal to you, there are also prepared foods available—chicken shawarma, piping hot pita, stuffed grape leaves, baklava, and the like are the ultimate comfort food. As if the 24-hour convenience and awesome selection of goods aren't enough, there's even a barber shop and bookstore on premises.

Specialty Stores, Markets & Producers

Crispy Sweetie, University City; 434 S. 52nd St., Philadelphia, PA 19143; (215) 472-6065; Doughnuts; $. Owner and confection genius Gyeong Moon may very well be University City's version of Willy Wonka—except for the fact that she's female and plies her trade in popcorn as well as candy. Her concept is so simple, it's amazing that there aren't more shops like hers. The specialty here is all things sweet—doughnuts, cakes, brownies and the like. The sweet/salty kettle corn—the kind that usually draws huge crowds at carnivals and state fairs—is highly addictive. While the bakery sweets are certainly a draw, it's the sweet glazed popcorn in flavors like grape, blue raspberry, caramel, cinnamon, and chocolate that will have you dancing like a kid in a candy store. Savory choices include jalapeño, sour cream, and cheese and are no less note-worthy. For those who long for the sweets of yesteryear, there's an assortment of old-school candy and gum. In addition, a limited assortment of imported, hard-to-find treats like Japanese Pocky, Meiji fruit candy, cookies, and Asian shrimp crackers are stocked for true snack diehards. The snacks are perfect for parties and Moon will gladly fill custom orders.

International Foods and Spices, University City; 4203 Walnut St., Philadelphia, PA 19104; (215) 222-4480; Specialty Grocery/International; $. To its credit, this University City section of

Philadelphia resembles a mini United Nations and is home to many ethnic restaurants and specialty stores. Unassuming from the outside and tucked next to a convenience store, this market is a specialty grocery shopper's dream. There's a plethora of Pakistani, Indian, and Middle Eastern products and grocery items. Chutneys, dried lentils, ghee (clarified butter), curry powder, spices, and dried nuts and fruit grace the shelves along with a number of hard-to-find,  foreign imports. There seems to be no rhyme or reason to the layout of the store and the offerings change frequently. If you're not keen on cooking then the prepared foods and frozen food section are great alternatives to the dry-goods aisle. There are snacks like samosas, falafel, and pakora ready for takeout.

P&P Grocery, University City; 4307 Locust St., Philadelphia, PA 19104; (215) 387-3509; Specialty Grocery; $. You could very well spend all day wandering through this hole-in-the-wall specialty market, not because of its square footage (which isn't much) but because there are a number of oddities and unusual products that warrant some extra perusing. There's an array of canned goods, ramen noodles, oils, curry pastes, and sauces for those looking to whip up pad thai and other Asian dishes at home. Tofu made in-house is insanely inexpensive and sold in individual squares—perfect for soups and stir-fries. Nonmeat eaters can come here for canned "mock meats" like mock duck and seitan, although sometimes they're not in stock. The owners, a husband and wife team, are so sweet and helpful in explaining some of the hard-to-recognize items and will even offer advice on cooking and preparation methods.

Rice-N-Spice International Grocery Store, University City; 4205 Chestnut St., Philadelphia, PA 19104; (215) 387-5250; Specialty Grocery/International; $. Walking through this West Philly specialty store feels much like a stroll through some remote spice market—Indian staples like rice, chai, spices, and a number of dry goods are fairly inexpensive. The real treasure here is the hidden restaurant, though. Partially hidden by a shelf and tucked away in the back of the grocery store and outfitted with the kind of fluorescent lights one might find in a questioning room in a police station, there is a dining hall of sorts frequented mostly by Punjabi immigrants and Indian students from the nearby university. Fancy it is not. It is beyond no-frills—the place is practically self-serve. The sole menu is written on a board tacked to the wall and diners are given a piece of paper to write down their orders which, in turn, they hand to a server. At first glance, the gathering of people hunched over Styrofoam plates of tandoori chicken and what looks like buckets of silken *paneer* and coriander-inflected *dhal,* looks like a secret supper club. However, Chef-Owner Jasvir Singh wants the space to be anything but—he subscribes to the "more the merrier" philosophy and wants everyone to be in on his "secret." If you're seeking something lighter and more portable, samosas that are sold for less than a dollar are a great choice.

Sips & the City

"Beer is proof that God loves us and wants us to be happy," is a line often attributed to Philadelphia's most famous kite flyer Benjamin Franklin. While sticklers for accuracy and historians often debate whether or not Franklin actually said it, one thing is undeniable: Philadelphians love their libations.

The city is full of craft breweries, pubs, and bars where brewmasters and mustachioed mixologists are treated like rock stars. This is the place where the tapping of the beer known as Pliny the Younger is a major frenzy-inducing event and cocktail loyalists count their favorite barkeeps/mixologists among their closest confidantes. Gastropubs, where the grub is just as revered as the drinks, have also garnered a huge following thanks to foodies and imbibers alike. Whether it's whiskey, beer, wine, or a cocktail, there's plenty of sipping going on in the city.

The Bards, 2013 Walnut St., Philadelphia, PA 19103; (215) 569-9585; bardsirishbar.com. In a city full of Irish pubs—some authentic and some not so much—The Bards feels like the real deal. Stepping inside is like a trip to Dublin; you half expect Oscar Wilde to be brooding in the corner over a pint. Sidle up to the bar during happy hour and score inexpensive drink specials. The affable (mostly Irish) staff at this quaint pub add to the overall appeal; heed the servers' advice when they suggest the Guinness Irish stew—a braised beef and root vegetable affair with fresh thyme and mashed potatoes. A menu of Irish standards (think shepherd's pie and bangers and mash) as well as some traditional American pub hits (chicken wings and tenders, burgers, and sandwiches) is well executed. A limited offering of gluten-free options in addition to a gluten-free beer option is available. Weekends are a grand affair with brunch and a pretty substantial DIY Bloody Mary bar with all the fixings.

Coco's, Market East; 112 S. 8th St., Philadelphia, PA 19107; (215) 923-0123. The largely undiscovered spot remains one of those familiar-yet-unfamiliar places that you vaguely remember walking past dozens of times but never crossed the threshold. Somehow, the place has managed to keep the Center City hipster set at bay—for now. It won't be long before word is out about the awesome drink specials (vodka lemonade, anyone?), juicy burgers, and the signature beer-battered onion rings, causing the masses to descend upon this tucked-away gem.

The Dandelion, 124 S. 18th St., Philadelphia, PA 19103; (215) 558-2500; thedandelionpub.com. Stephen Starr's ode to the Union Jack resonates with the city's expats and admiring Anglophiles alike. There's no shortage of British pubs, but somehow this pub manages to differentiate itself from the rest of its ilk. From the dark woods to the knick-knacks dotted around the dining room, this is illusion at its finest, representing what über-restaurateur Starr does best. Snack on deviled eggs or Welsh rarebit on buttermilk toast before segueing into prawns served with a lemony mayonnaise. If you're game for game, consider the rabbit pie with oyster mushrooms and smoked bacon. Get your monarch on and imagine you're at a cricket match while sipping on a Pimm's Cup (or Pimm's Deluxe) or the Bombardier Shandy. If boozy beverages aren't your thing, opt for one of Luscombe's authentic bottled sodas or a Fentiman's tonic.

Johnny Brenda's, Fishtown; 1201 Frankford Ave., Philadelphia, PA 19125; (215) 739-9684; johnnybrendas.com. Neighborhood favorite Johnny Brenda's is owned by the same folks who own **Standard Tap** (pp. 60, 191) and has completely endeared itself to the area's hipsters and music lovers. It's part gastropub, part music venue, where the taps are plentiful and the cask ale flows freely; a decent liquor and wine list is available as well. JB's also prides itself on offering a selection of local beers. The menu of local and seasonal snacks and elevated pub grub is creative and well executed, but a simple burger and fries are just as enjoyable.

Khyber Pass Pub, Old City; 56 S. 2nd St., Philadelphia, PA 19106; (215) 238-5888; khyberpasspub.com. Three words: bacon grease popcorn. Really, those should be the only words necessary to get you running to Khyber Pass Pub, but, alas, you may need more convincing. The pub itself is a strange breed—at any given moment, blood-curdling heavy metal may be pumping from the sound system but the menu is full of down-home comfort food with a Cajun/Creole slant. The beer selection is plentiful and, while there are some recognizable popular bottles, it includes mainly microbrews. The barely lit dining area is the perfect place to enjoy a brew and the popular smoked cheddar fries topped with debris gravy—a tasty gravy made from shredded meat (typically roast beef) and its pan juices.

London Grill, Fairmount; 2301 Fairmount Ave., Philadelphia, PA 19130; (215) 978-4545; londongrill.com. A menu of unpretentious and delicious pub food, a limited but carefully selected draft list and a staff-created cocktail menu make this neighborhood staple a favorite haunt of the Fairmount crowd. Prep your palate with Pernod-spiked baked escargots or the earthy roasted beet Napoleon with goat cheese and blood orange. Filling mains like the roasted duck with port-cherry compote and house-made pastas aim to satisfy larger appetites.

Memphis Taproom, Kensington; 2331 E. Cumberland St., Philadelphia, PA 19125; (215) 425-4460; memphistaproom.com. With 10 draft beers (and a beer engine), a menu of elevated pub fare, and an outdoor hot dog and fried pickle truck, this Kensington bar has steadily climbed the ranks over the years to become one of the city's top pubs. It's the perfect place to kick back and enjoy a brew; don't skip the beer garden out back—it's a must-do in warmer months. The beer selection is praiseworthy as is the menu of throwbacks like pierogies and bratwurst that offer a deferential nod to the Polish-heavy neighborhood; expect surprises in the form of smoked coconut tofu club or the chicken-fried portobello sandwich; kick your palate into high gear with an order of suicide rings with habañero cream.

Resurrection Ale House, Grays Ferry/Graduate Hospital; 2425 Grays Ferry Ave., Philadelphia, PA 19146; resurrectionalehouse.com. This gastropub claims prime real estate across the street from the gargantuan Naval Square condominium complex. The popular craft beer bar/restaurant may be a tried-and-true neighborhood staple, but there's always something surprising cropping up on the appetizing menu of little bites (try the chicory salad), sandwiches like the goat cheese and speck with fig jam and arugula, or the twice-fried chicken—a cult favorite bolstered by a spicy honey glaze and

German-style potato salad. A dozen or so beers, including those from local favorites Dogfish Head Brewery (Milton, DE) and Sly Fox (Phoenixville, PA) are on tap daily with special cask ale usually making an appearance as well.

Royal Tavern, Bella Vista; 937 E. Passyunk Ave., Philadelphia, PA 19147; (215) 389-6694; royaltavern.com. As expected, weekends here can get hectic as the drinking set clamors for their liquid comfort, which undoubtedly will have them indulging in one of city's best Bloody Mary bars to cure their hangovers. In contrast, the weekdays are pretty tame and subdued enough to actually hear oneself think, though you may find yourself waiting for a table during peak hours. It is a rarity indeed to find a bar with such an extensive vegan/vegetarian menu, but those with carnivorous tendencies shouldn't despair; the legendary Angus burger with caramelized onions, smoked Gouda, and pickled long hots isn't going anywhere. Also see main listing on p. 149.

South Philadelphia Taproom, Newbold; 1509 Mifflin St., Philadelphia, PA 19145; (215) 271-7787; southphiladelphiataproom .com. After nearly 10 years in business, this South Philly favorite takes pride in the fact that it's not a Belgian bar nor does it carry imports—this is American beer at its finest. There are 14 rotating taps and approximately 75 to 100 bottled beers; the draft list features selections from some of Philadelphia's finest breweries. A

menu of comforting hit-the-spot classics like a buttery grilled cheese sandwich with tomato lager soup and hearty meat loaf with a surprise side of barbecued mushrooms serve as a perfect foil.

Watkins Drinkery, Bella Vista; 1712 S. 10th St., Philadelphia, PA 19148; (215) 339-0175. At first glance, this place seems more befitting of the frat-boy set but to write it off as simply a playground for rowdy youngsters isn't fair. Watkins Drinkery is the sister bar to The Dive; thankfully, owner John Klein created Watkins with a more mature feel than its counterpart. The pub won't win any awards for decor to be sure, but absent are the cheap beers, TVs permanently tuned to the cartoon channel, and the less-than-lackluster menu. With a completely unapologetic and adventurous menu, this place is a serious contender among the pool of gastropubs in the city. If you're looking for a typical burger and fries joint, you'd do well to frequent any number of the city's cookie-cutter bars. This is the place where you can nosh on alligator, ostrich, and other nontraditional meats in familiar, more recognizable offerings. Here, nachos shrug off their boring pub-grub reputation and get topped with venison or kangaroo—yes, kangaroo. Six taps pour mostly local and craft beers and a pulled quail sandwich accompanied by a perfectly complementary beer can be enjoyed while watching some hometown baseball or, if you're of the nonmeat-eating variety, try the vegan cheese-topped "meatball" (vegball?) sandwich—a favorite even the carnivorous can appreciate. If you're feeling nostalgic, head upstairs to the old-school game room where a pool table and vintage video games from the '80s live; there's also a small bar for escapists looking to chill.

Suds

Eulogy Belgian Tavern, Old City; 136 Chestnut St., Philadelphia, PA 19106; eulogybar.com. Housed in a historic 2-story row house, Eulogy is anything but dead. The popular Belgian tavern features an impressive 21 taps and 300 different bottled beers. An award-winning menu (try the burger made with seven secret spices and the double-fried Flemish-style fries) and a few visa-toting Belgian employees make this Old City watering hole a prime destination as evidenced by the number of awards it consistently wins year after year. Though it's a bit hokey, try snagging a table upstairs in the appropriately-cramped "coffin room," where tables are replaced with caskets and patrons can enjoy snacks and suds in an—er—intimate setting.

The Foodery, Northern Liberties; 837 N. 2nd St., Philadelphia, PA 19123; (215) 238-6077; fooderybeer.com. It's no secret that Philadelphians love beer, so it's only natural that this Northern Liberties beer emporium (technically, it's not a bar) attracts suds lovers from all over the city. Enthusiasts can shop for local labels from Yards or popular Dogfish Head Brewery as well as foreign bottles. The selection of more than 800 American and imported craft beers is available by the bottle or you can build your own customized carryout six-pack. There's also an on-site deli that serves up hoagies, sandwiches, and panini, making The Foodery the perfect place to grab some suds and a sammie. If you're always on the lookout for new beers or want to familiarize yourself with old standards, consider attending one of the samplings offered several times a month; check the website for a complete schedule. Additional location at 324 S. 10th St., Philadelphia, PA 19107.

Frankford Hall, Northern Liberties/Fishtown; 1210 Frankford Ave., Philadelphia, PA 19125; frankfordhall.com. This epic beer garden pays homage to their German equivalents with a varied selection of on-tap and craft beers. A filling snack menu of warm pretzels, spaetzle, sausages (a bratwurst with kraut or red cabbage is a must), and burgers complete the experience. Don't expect the reasonably priced half- and full-liter beers to be served by strolling Bavarian barmaids, though—patrons purchase food and drinks from walk-up vendors who line the perimeter of the courtyard. Crowds flock here for the beer and the packed social calendar, full of events like s'mores roastings during the cooler months and the popular "Nerd Nite."

The Grey Lodge Pub, Tacony; 6235 Frankford Ave., Philadelphia, PA 19135; (215) 856-3591; greylodge.com. This friendly Northeast pub has a bit of a personality disorder—the good kind, that is. The bilevel space's first floor can be rowdy (especially when sporting events are being televised), music-filled, and often packed to the rafters, which makes chatting up a stranger at the oval bar easy. The second floor is dedicated to a family-friendly dining room and  is a tad more polished and quieter. Don't worry—that doesn't mean you can't grab a drink up there; there's a small bar with a stellar beer and whiskey selection comparable to that of the first floor. They're no slouches on food here, either. You'll find standard pub food in addition to their famous ode-to-Philly steak (try the sliced rib-eye cheesesteak) and roast pork sandwiches (get the Italiano). Thanks to an amusement permit, there are games and electronic darts should the need to engage in competitive sports hit you; a jam-packed jukebox ups the entertainment factor.

José Pistolas, Rittenhouse Square; 263 S. 15th St., Philadelphia, PA 19102; (215) 545-4101; josepistolas.com. This Tex-Mex bar is a total wildcard; you'd hardly expect a casual Mexican restaurant to have such an extensive and carefully curated beer selection. The constantly rotating draft list offers everything from hard cider to local favorite Yards Love Stout; the bottled beer selection reads like a veritable who's-who with dozens of labels rounding out the list. As far as the menu goes, there are no real surprises; everything is classical Tex-Mex. Tacos, burritos, sandwiches, and starters make for good bites as do the more filling entrees.

Local 44, University City; 4333 Spruce St., Philadelphia, PA 19104; (215) 222-2337; local44beerbar.com. Considered by some to have the best draft list in the city, this University City bar (the folks here cringe at the mere thought of being called a gastropub) is a breath of fresh air for the West Philadelphia bar scene that's been on life support for years. On the weekends, count on having to elbow your way to the bar or risk leaving thirsty. Tastefully selected, the beer list (written on a blackboard) is impeccable but nearly impossible to read from any table that is more than a few feet away. While there are more than a dozen beers on tap, there's only one bottled beer offered—albeit a great one (Orval Trappist Ale) which is never available on draft. Bottle lovers need not worry—Local 44 operates a bottle shop down the street with more 500 labels available to drink in-store or on the go. The beer-appropriate menu of hits like chile sauce–glazed "sticky" wings and a garlic mustard–slathered kielbasa sandwich offer solid sustenance.

McNally's Tavern, Chestnut Hill; 8634 Germantown Ave., Philadelphia, PA 19118; (215) 247-9736; mcnallystavern.com. Located at the "top of the hill" in suburban Chestnut Hill, McNally's is a longstanding landmark. The pub is a cozy neighborhood haunt where the signature sandwiches tend to overshadow the beer list, which is decent but not too exotic. You won't find a bunch of craft brews, but you will find the world-famous phenomenon known as The Schmitter—a monstrous (and sloppy) cheesesteak hybrid with grilled salami,

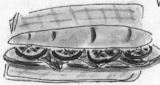

tomatoes, cheese, and fried onions slathered with a special sauce on a toasted Kaiser roll. The sandwich is so popular that it's actually been trademarked; it even makes an appearance at the concession stands of major sporting venues.

Monk's Cafe, Rittenhouse Square; 264 S. 16th St., Philadelphia, PA 19146; (215) 545-7005; monkscafe.com. A few years ago, Philadelphia caught the Belgian craze. No, there weren't crowds spilling into the streets demanding chocolate—it was beer they sought. Now, there are several cafes and bars in the city that serve (and celebrate) Belgian suds. Monk's, however, distinguishes itself from the rest of the pack with an impressive list of awards and accolades like its 2011 distinction as one of the Top Five Beer Trailblazers by *Wine Enthusiast* magazine. Both novices and beer snobs can learn a thing or two from the cafe's "beer bible"—an exhaustive compilation of more than 200 beers complete with informative tidbits about production and taste. Suds are bountiful here, with the front and back bars housing more than 20 rotating taps and a dynamite variety of cellared beers. Fear not, foodies—just because the beer enjoys the spotlight doesn't mean the menu suffers. Not one bit. Widely thought to be one of the most underrated menus in the area, Monk's serves up noteworthy plates of *pommes frites* (the bourbon aioli is divine), grilled scallops (with a beurre blanc crafted from private label Flemish sour ale), and a bowl-licking gaggle of mussels (try the Saison Dupont–simmered Ghent mussels with bacon, blue cheese, fumet, and caramelized leeks). If you're looking to learn more about the inner workings of the cafe, looking to beef up your knowledge of beer, or are interested in learning about beer pairings, Monk's regularly hosts tours and dinners. Visit the website for more information; early booking is recommended.

Nodding Head Brewery & Restaurant, Rittenhouse Square; 1516 Sansom St., Philadelphia, PA 19102; (215) 569-9525; nodding head.com. You can often tell what season it is by what's on tap at Nodding Head; the ever-changing list offers selections ranging from Tasman to Grog to seasonal Spring Ale. By far, the most popular beer is the giggle-inducing Asian-spiced blonde lager known as **Monkey Knife Fight** (p. 104); the menu of burgers, sandwiches, and small tapas-like bites are delicious, but the real draw is the mussels that come in the "black and blue," "jerked," and Moroccan varieties. A delicious brunch flies under the radar, giving those in the know the run of the place on the weekends.

Oscar's Tavern, Rittenhouse Square; 1524 Sansom St., Philadelphia, PA 19102; (215) 972-9938. Nondescript, dingy, and a complete dive, Oscar's is the kind of place that may inspire you to get a tetanus shot after visiting. Ironically, that's part of the overall charm and appeal of this bar—that and the hangover-inducing, cheap (but huge) 23-ounce beer pours. This place stands in sharp contrast to the prototypical, overpriced Center City bar scene despite its rather trendy address. The crowd here is an odd mix of cash-strapped college students, strange characters, and people looking for a cheap night out on the town. Leave your pretentiousness at home—there's no artful craft beer list (although Dogfish Head or Victory beer occasionally make an appearance) and the bartender won't bore you with a spiel about how the beer was produced or present a case on subtle nuancing of flavor. The fanciest thing in the place is the jukebox filled to the brim with a mix of music eclectic enough to keep the equally diverse crowd happy. At Oscar's, you can get down and dirty—not unlike the bar itself. Cash only.

Sidecar Bar & Grille, Graduate Hospital; 2201 Christian St., Philadelphia, PA 19146; (215) 732-3429; thesidecarbar.com. A meticulously crafted beer list presents a host of choices for hops junkies (including gluten-free options) and rotates frequently. The vibe is fun and homey—all boosting its neighborhood-gem quotient. Sidecar gets major props for having two happy hours—the first of which is held from 3 to 7 p.m. and a late-night one from midnight to 2 a.m. As an added bonus, if you can prove you work in the restaurant biz, you're entitled to happy hour discounts all day, every day. The dinner menu is a greatest hits of sorts that's full of pub faves like crispy, sauce-slathered chicken wings, pork nachos, and steamed PEI mussels. Don't miss the notable burgers—especially the one topped with a poached egg, gruyère, and truffle mayo.

Standard Tap, Northern Liberties; 901 N. 2nd St., Philadelphia, PA 19123; (215) 238-0630; standardtap.com. Replete with reimagined tavern fare, the menu is full of standouts; couple that with a stellar beer selection and it's easy to see why it's a perennial favorite. This gastropub draws a diverse crowd—musicians, hipsters, businesspeople, loyalists, and newcomers come together to show this place some love. See main listing, p. 60.

Vino & Cocktails

Agiato, Roxborough/Manayunk, 4359 Main St., Philadelphia, PA 19127; (215) 482-9700; agiatophila.com; Wine Bar. A wine list and local beer roster attracts oenophiles and hops heads alike to this Manayunk neighborhood favorite. Sip on a glass of wine from the Italian, French, or Spanish list while enjoying crostini or antipasti from the European-inspired menu. See main listing, p. 28.

Bar Ferdinand, Northern Liberties; 1030 N. 2nd St., Philadelphia, PA 19123; (215) 923-1313; barferdinand.com; Wine Bar. Looking every bit like a Spanish count's villa, an elegant 20-seat wraparound bar is stylish yet inviting. Nurse your inner matador at this NoLibs tapas-style restaurant, whose list of 50 Spanish wines (25 of which are available by the glass) is impressive and well thought out, as is the beer list. Both the red and white varieties of sangria are the perfect start to a meal of authentic tapas like *croquetas* or empanadas. See main listing, p. 29.

Caribou Cafe, Market East; 1126 Walnut St., Philadelphia, PA 19107; (215) 625-9535; cariboucafe.com; Cocktails. There are plenty of places for Francophiles to eat and drink around the city, but many are stuffy, pretentious, and not conducive to having a casual night out with friends over a drink (or three). Caribou Cafe has one of the most relaxed atmospheres around— no doubt enhanced by the smooth jazz music wafting through the restaurant. Bistro classics like *steak-frites* and artisanal cheese plates are authentic and crafted to pair with impres-  sive wine and beer lists that feature 22 wines by the glass and 40 specialty beers along with—not surprisingly—a host of classic French aperitifs and cocktails.

Chick's Social Kitchen & Bar, Bella Vista; 614 S. 7th St., Philadelphia, PA 19147; (215) 625-3700; chickssocial.net; Wine Bar. There are plenty residents who remember Chick's Cafe as one of the area's premier wine bars. In its latest incarnation, the nearly 120-year-old stalwart has evolved into a refined restaurant with an Italian farmhouse menu. Don't worry—the carefully selected wine list is still intact and offers crisp whites and robust reds. Suds seekers won't be disappointed with the draft and bottle list, either. The sips are complemented by small bites, an array of antipasti (try the hand-selected charcuterie and cheese board) and panini. Larger groups looking to delve into something more substantial should consider The Timpano—a massive pasta pie filled with sausage, sharp provolone, Tuscan salami, hard-boiled eggs and (as hard as it is to believe), a host of other ingredients.

Continental Midtown, Rittenhouse Square; 1801 Chestnut St., Philadelphia, PA 19103; (215) 567-1800; continentalmidtown .com; Cocktails. This chic martini bar features three floors with a rooftop dining area and partially enclosed lounge area that allows for year-round service. A deck area is perfect for enjoying drinks during the warmer months. Young hipsters can nosh on favorites like the lobster mac and cheese, crab pad thai, and Korean pork tacos while sipping on throwback cocktails (try the Old Fashioned with house-cured cherries). Fun, modern sips like the Sourpuss count St. Germain elderflower liqueur and sour candy among their ingredients. Brunch here is a perennial favorite and has been dishing up eye-opening eats to hangover nursers and trendy foodies for years.

The Farmers' Cabinet, Market East; 1113 Walnut St., Philadelphia, PA 19107; (215) 923-1113; thefarmerscabinet.com; Cocktails. Sea salt–flecked bone marrow and a warm, buttery Bavarian pretzel are typical of the small bites offered. Foodies may flock to this Center City eatery for its ode-to-rustic-American menu, but the cocktail-obsessed clamor for a seat at this mixology haven. An artful—and pleasantly intellectual—cocktail list often draws inspirations from music or literature. The Flames of Troy, a bourbon-based drink spiked with ginger beer, pays tribute to Shakespeare's *Julius Caesar*.

The Franklin Mortage & Investment Company, Rittenhouse Square; 112 S. 18th St., 1st Fl.; Philadelphia, PA 19103; thefranklin bar.com; Cocktails. Cocktail nerds rejoice—strikingly well-informed bartenders possess encyclopedic knowledge of all things liquid and serve, arguably, the best cocktails in the city. Conjuring up memories of the Prohibition Era, the underground speakeasy exudes an air of exclusivity, as if you've been let into a secret society. Though the creatively named drinks utilize ingredients that range from the approachable to the downright confusing, half the fun is getting a primer in green chartreuse liqueur, Xocolatl mole bitters, or the merits of using demerara sugar. This place is for the serious connoisseur and there are rules—no loitering around the bar (you must be seated or you must wait in line) and absolutely no vodka. If an energy drink and vodka mixture is your poison of choice, you'd do well to patronize another establishment.

Il Bar, Old City; 14 N. Front St., Philadelphia, PA 19106; (215) 922-7800; pennsviewhotel.com; Wine Bar. Located in the boutique Penn's View Hotel, this chic oenophile charmer serves as the companion bar to Ristorante Panorama—the hotel's first-floor Italian trattoria. A colossal cruvinet system, recognized by the Guinness World Records as the "largest wine preservation and dispensing system in the world," allows for the tapping of rare and expensive wines that are not normally available by the glass. The intricate system uses gas to prevent oxidation and spoilage and exposes casual sippers to a whole new level of fine wines. The entire setup is quite impressive and you could literally spend half the night staring at the display, but the idea is to drink the wine not stare at it. Flights are available in five 1.5-ounce pours and offer an excellent opportunity to embrace (or dismiss) wines from various regions around the world. Don't be intimidated by the swank setting or intricate workings as the wines are completely approachable and the staff is helpful in their recommendations. Beautifully prepared antipasti, salads, and pastas (available in half or full portions) pair perfectly with the rotating wine list as well as the creative cocktail menu.

Jake & Cooper's Wine Bar, Manayunk; 4365 Main St., Philadelphia, PA 19127; (215) 483-0444; Wine Bar. This friendly, casual wine bar is located on Manayunk's main drag and has a great selection of wines and beers—all appropriately complementary to New American cuisine of sandwiches and brick-oven pizzas. Given the atmosphere, this is the kind of place where you'd want to meet up with friends and share some plates over one (or two) glasses.

Meritage, 500 S. 20th St., Rittenhouse Square; Philadelphia, PA 19146; (215) 985-1922; meritagephiladelphia.com; Wine Bar. Not far from ritzy Rittenhouse Square, Meritage is a fine diner's (drinker's) paradise. An approachable seasonal menu meshes well with a well-thought-out, though pricey, wine list. See main listing, p. 86.

Oyster House, Rittenhouse Square; 1516 Sansom St., Philadelphia, PA 19102; (215) 567-7683; oysterhousephilly.com; Cocktails. What's not to love at a place that offers a buck-a-shuck oyster-centric happy hour? The raw bar and cooked seafood options (think fried Ipswich clams and lobster rolls) will transport you to the coast with a classic-meets-modern cocktail menu that comes along for the ride. Oyster aficionados who like to mix their liquor and mollusks will appreciate the succinct menu of oyster shooters; try downing the hot pepper and cilantro vodka–infused Chihuahua.

Parc, Rittenhouse Square; 227 S. 18th St., Philadelphia, PA 19103; (215) 545-2262; parc-restaurant.com; Cocktails. Parisian fantasies come true at the über-posh Parc, where the drinks may be expensive but the ambience assuages the nerves of those who take issue with hefty price tags. An exhaustive list features more than 160 wines that are available by the bottle with more than 20 available by the glass. An equally extensive cocktail menu is impressive.

Ranstead Room, Rittenhouse Square; 2013 Ranstead St., Philadelphia, PA 19103; (215) 563-3330; Cocktails. At first glance, Ranstead Room is yet another bar whose cocktail list nods to the Prohibition Era. Semi-hidden doors emblazoned with "RR" may seem kitschy and contrived, but all is forgiven once you pass through a second set of double doors and are taken in by the subtle elegance and the crew of skillful mixologists who concoct a bevy of inventive libations.

Southwark, Queen Village; 701 S. 4th St., Philadelphia, PA 19147; (215) 238-1888; southwarkrestaurant.com; Cocktails. It's often hard to justify a $15 cocktail, but you'll hardly notice the price tag once you sip one of the creations—even the classic drinks are well executed. An oh-so-serious commitment to serving authentic farm-to-table fare is evident in the menu of fresh, eclectic bistro preparations. See main listing, p. 146.

Tinto, Rittenhouse Square; 114 S. 20th St., Philadelphia, PA 19103; (215) 665-9150; tintorestaurant.com; Wine Bar. Iron Chef José Garces pays homage to the coastal region between Spain and France known as Basque country with an extensive wine list of more than 100 varieties from both countries' wine-producing regions. The dark woods and Spanish-tiled floors lend to the ambience of the wine cellar–like space, while the 22-foot-long bar inspires languid drink sipping and conversation. Weather permitting, take advantage of alfresco dining when the floor-to-ceiling glass doors are thrown open and views of 20th Street are ideal for people-watching.

Tria, Rittenhouse Square & Washington Square West; 123 S. 18th St., Philadelphia, PA 19103 and 1137 Spruce St., Philadelphia, PA 19107; (215) 972-8742; triacafe .com; Wine Bar. Wine lovers, craft beer enthusiasts and cheese aficionados gather at this James Beard Award–winning wine bar over glasses of luscious whites and spicy reds and approachable brews. Sleek and sophisticated, Tria draws an equally sophisticated crowd of hipsters who come to socialize and nosh on small plates of snacks, bruschetta, salads, and panini. A knowledgeable but unpretentious staff is always willing to offer spot-on suggestions to both novices and experts. See main listing, p. 97.

Vino Volo, Southwest Philadelphia; 8500 Essington Ave., Philadelphia, PA 19153; (215) 365-8600; vinovolo.com; Wine Bar. First things first: Yes, Vino Volo is a—gasp—chain. Secondly, it is located in an airport. Once you wrap your head around those two facts, you'll realize that it ranks as one of the best wine bars in the city and that's no small feat. With various locations dotted around the terminals at Philadelphia International Airport, Vino Volo continues to shock (and wow) skeptical travelers with a thoughtful menu of bar fare (the brie and prosciutto sandwich is divine) and a more-than-decent selection of domestic and world wines; wine flights offer respectable samplings. The price ranges can vary wildly—from a reasonable $9 per glass to an unthinkable $30 per glass for one of the fancier labels, but really who can complain about a place that allows you to escape the chaos of a busy airport with a simple glass of vino?

Vintage Wine Bar and Bistro, Market East; 129 S. 13th St., Philadelphia, PA 19176; (215) 922-3095; vintage-philadelphia.com; Wine Bar. More than 60 wines by the glass and about 25 bottles grace the extensive list at this Center City gem. Pore over the list and select a lusty red or remove indecisiveness from the equation and order one of the wine flights, which consist of three 3-ounce pours. A European-inspired menu of elevated bar food like brie *en* *croûte* or the sweet/savory Gorgonzola and fig bruschetta harmonize well with the meticulously crafted wine list and make for a delicious pairing.

Zahav, Society Hill; 237 St. James Pl., Philadelphia, PA 19106; (215) 625-8800; zahavrestaurant.com; Cocktails. Highly underrated, Zahav is home to one of the best bars around. Jerusalem-inspired *salatim,* a variety of hummus, and imaginative reinterpretations of classics are balanced by not only a thoughtful list of Israeli wines but also a concise offering of flat-out sexy cocktails (try the New Jerusalem Cocktail). The bright and slightly tart Lemonnana, a mélange of Jim Beam, fresh lemon, muddled mint, and verbena, is the ideal foil especially to the spicier menu items. See main listing, p. 101.

Zavino, Midtown Village; 112 S. 13th St., Philadelphia, PA 19107; (215) 732-2400; zavino.com; Wine Bar. Pizza and beer may very well be the most perfect food and drink combination known to man—it's hard to argue against the pairing of a chile-flake-flecked Berkshire pork sausage and provolone pie and some local suds. A menu of small plates (think house-cured olives and oven-roasted brussels sprouts) and a cheese selection that ranges from earthy to sharp to pungent rounds out the offerings.

Farm Fresh

Years ago, the notion of eating processed, preservative-laden food was out of the question—if you didn't grow it or raise it, you didn't eat it. Luckily, there has been an overwhelming return to the land and the regional locavore movement is becoming more prevalent as people begin to say goodbye to the endless grocery store aisles and imported produce. Finally, the general population is catching on to what farmers have known for centuries—without farms, there is no real food. Chefs are aware of this fact as well, and their menus now often disclose the provenance of their ingredients and highlight local farms, farmers, and purveyors. From breeding heritage animals to cultivating heirloom seeds, local farmers are responsible for providing the most stellar meats and produce for the area's best chefs and restaurants.

For more in-depth information on local CSAs (community supported agriculture), buying clubs, farmers' markets, and the local-eating movement, visit Farm to City's website at **farmtocity.org.**

Chestnut Hill Growers' Market (year-round), Winston Road (between Germantown Avenue and Mermaid Lane); farmtocity.org. Highlights at this year-round suburban market include chemical-free organic fruits and vegetables, goat milk, yogurt, and artisanal cheeses. Local honey and sustainably caught fish as well as gluten-free bread and decadent *canelés* round out the list of edible delights.

Clark Park Farmers' Market (year-round), University City; 43rd Street & Baltimore Avenue, Philadelphia, PA 19143; ucityphila .org. The park hosts Philadelphia's largest year-round farmers' market and offers seasonal produce (both organic and conventional) as well as beef, chicken, lamb, pork, veal, honey, goat cheese and milk, maple syrup, canned goods, baked goods, and fresh-cut flowers. Highlights include artisanal chocolates from local favorite John & Kira's, grass-fed beef from Landisdale Farm, and delicious gluten-free breads and sweets from Amaranth Gluten-Free Bakery. After shopping, be sure to stop by Yumtown, USA—a seasonal food truck that dishes up fanciful bites like PB&J *tostones* made with pork belly, pumpkin butter, and chile jam. Adding to the list of mobile food trucks that often set down temporary roots in Clark Park, Honest Tom's Taco Truck often stops by to offer its now-famous tacos and breakfast burritos to the hungry masses.

Gorgas Park Farmers' Market (seasonal), 6400 Ridge Ave. Philadelphia, PA 19128; farmtocity.org. Having undergone a major revitalization years ago and shaking off its old image as a dilapidated hangout, Gorgas Park has functioned as the heartbeat and pride of the urban community of Roxborough for quite some time. A remarkable bounty of fresh garden fruits and vegetables along with honey, vegetable and herb seedlings, and cider is the handiwork of Marc Wilken of McCann's Farm of Elk Township in Gloucester County, New Jersey.

Fountain Farmers' Market (seasonal), East Passyunk Avenue at 11th & Tasker Streets; farmtocity.org. Glorious bouquets of fresh-cut flowers and herbs reside alongside produce, cheese, eggs, honey, and locally made preserves from specialty market **Green Aisle Grocery** (p. 155). Fruit and vegetable breads and Amish baked goods are a huge draw as well.

Greensgrow Farm (year-round), Fishtown; 2501 E. Cumberland St., Philadelphia, PA 19125; (215) 427-2702; greensgrow.org. It's hard to imagine anything green thriving within the concrete confines of the Fishtown/Kensington area, never mind actual farmland. Greensgrow is an anomaly of sorts and sticks out like a sore (albeit green) thumb—in a good way, of course. It operates a farm stand that brings together area purveyors and producers and presents a beautiful mash-up of some of the finest and freshest food in the city. Linvilla Orchards and Gaventa's Farm are contributors and tomatoes from Lancaster County are always a hit. Greensgrow's basil plants are legendary and find themselves worked into a wonderful pesto that is among its bestsellers. It's easy to get lost in the ruffled leaves of tender greens or be mesmerized by the brightly hued produce, but to do so would mean that you'd miss out on Lancaster County free-range eggs, silken whole-milk yogurt, sweet cream butter and wedges of artisanal cheeses. Joining the CSA makes supplementing your groceries easy; sign up for a half or whole share and enjoy a seasonal assortment of locally grown veg-

 etables and fruits from outlying farms as well as yogurt, cheese, and farm-fresh, cage-free eggs. Participants eschewing all things dairy can opt to substitute locally crafted seitan or tofu. CSA shares are occasionally bolstered by breads, apple cider, honey, fresh pasta, prepared foods, and even Kensington-produced beer from Philadelphia Brewing Company.

Headhouse Farmers Market (seasonal), Society Hill; South Street & S. 2nd Street, Philadelphia, PA 19147; foodtrustmarkets .org; Farmers Market; $$. Spring and summer bring the promise of not only warm weather, backyard barbecues, and outdoor activities, but also lazy weekends spent strolling farmers' markets. Forfeit a few hours of slumber on a weekend morning to get to this cash-only farmers' market early to beat the crowd; fill your baskets with earthy beets, tomatoes, local cheeses, and pastured eggs. Stock up on artisanal maple syrup, honey, and cider before indulging in the addictive cinnamon swirl bread from Ric's or the custardy *canelé* from Market Day Canelé; don't forget to get your meat fix from **Renaissance Sausage** (p. 109). While most people visit the market to snag ingredients for cooking, there are many visitors who would rather chow down on prepared foods (of which there is an abundant supply) and if you're one of them, feel free to grab a seat on the nearby steps and people-watch.

Rittenhouse Farmers' Market (year-round), 18th and Walnut Streets, Philadelphia, PA 19103; farmtocity.org. Braving the elements at this year-round market, the vendors who offer their wares to hoardes of shoppers are true weekend warriors. Bring a tote, a pushcart, and whatever else is necessary to haul away your purchases as resisting jewel-colored produce, pastured meat, scores of local dairy products, artisanal jams and preserves, and fresh-baked bread may prove difficult. Delicious baked goods from Amaranth Gluten-Free Bakery, earthy toothsome mushrooms from Davidson Exotics, and a selection of meats (especially the *guanciale*) from PorcSalt top the list of highlights. Given the location, prices tend to run on the higher side; if you are looking to purchase your entire grocery list here, be prepared to shell out some serious coin.

South & Passyunk Farmers' Market (seasonal), Passyunk Avenue, off of South Street and just east of 5th Street; farmtocity .org. At any given time, there are only about five vendors at this South Street–area farmers' market and, while their wares certainly help supplement one's grocery needs, the choices (as stellar as they may be) are extremely limited. However, what this producer-only market lacks in volume, it more than makes up for in quality.

Shortcomings are forgiven with farm-fresh eggs that put their store-bought cousins to shame, plus vibrant produce, and several cuts of meat; plants and herbs are the hallmarks of the market. Consider a delicious selection of breads as well, and a small offering of artisan chocolates and jellies. The tiny market gets less foot traffic than others in the area, which makes for a less chaotic shopping experience.

Suburban Station Farmers' Market (year-round), 16th Street at Market Street and JFK Boulevard; farmtocity.org. Named after the train station it's situated near, this metro market is the ideal stop for commuters looking to score fresh produce, pastured meats, and eggs in between rail rides.

University Square Farmers' Market (seasonal), 36th Street at Walnut Street; diningatpenn.com. Students and residents alike anxiously await Spring's arrival because it means the University of Pennsylvania's campus will once again host its seasonal farmers' market. Regular market vendors include Beechwood Orchards (selling locally grown fruit), John & Kira's (selling gourmet chocolates and hand-crafted confections), and Metropolitan Bakery (offering their famed breads, bagels, pastries, cookies, sandwiches, locally roasted coffees, and organic teas). Recently, a number of new additions have arrived—of note are Lancaster-based Amaranth Gluten-Free Bakery, Philadelphia's own Better Butter, whose all-natural peanut butter spreads are addictive, and McCann's Farm from Monroesville, NJ, whose bounty of tomatoes, sweet corn, blueberries, and melons are perfect ingredients for meals during the warmer months but, in actuality, are good enough to eat straight from the vendor.

Walnut Hill Farmstand (seasonal), 4610 Market St., Philadelphia, PA 19139; farmtophilly.com. Typically, metropolitan areas lack green space but there are some industrious growers who engage in urban farming, using what limited resources they have at their disposal. This particular farm stand is one of two operated by Walnut Hill Community Farm and is tended to by the program's young participants, known as "youth growers." As is customary, this farm stand doesn't have as much variety as a true farmers' market, but what is available—specifically pesticide- and herbicide-free vegetables—is delicious.

Suburban Gems

There is no denying that the city is teeming with fine eateries helmed by adventurous and creative chefs, but that creativity is not wholly confined within city limits. In years past, many scoffed at the idea of dining outside of the city; but the culinary landscape is growing by leaps and bounds and is spreading far outside the borders of Philadelphia. To dismiss the suburbs and other outlying areas as fine dining deserts is a mistake; there are a number of opportunities to experience delightful meals in areas far from the city's center.

Foodie Faves

Arpeggio, 1101 Bethlehem Pk., Spring House, PA 19477; (215) 646-5055; arpeggiobyob.com; Mediterranean; $$. At Arpeggio, pizza reigns supreme. A wood-burning oven turns out beautiful pies in the thin-crusted, regular, and whole wheat varieties with fresh, herb-flecked tomato sauce and dozens of topping possibilities. The Santorini is a nod to the Mediterranean with briny kalamata olives, red onions, and feta with a drizzle of fruity olive oil. Don't call Arpeggio a pizzeria, though. Pizza is just one facet of the extensive menu at this family-friendly, casual BYOB; it offers more than a dozen salads and just as many pastas, sandwiches, and grilled kebabs.

Blackfish, 119 Fayette St., Conshohocken, PA 19428; (610) 397-0888; blackfishrestaurant.com; New American; $$$. When word about this miniature BYOB first got out, city dwellers were skeptical. After all, it's located in a section of town known more for its casual concepts and pubs than haute cuisine, but a step inside Blackfish's dining room reveals clean, sharp lines and minimalist furnishing that exude a kind of quiet sophistication that would hold its own against any metropolis's eatery. Chef-Owner Charles "Chip" Roman's youth belies the complexity and refinement of his artistically created dishes as evidenced in his signature appetizer of an applewood smoked salmon–encased soft deep-fried egg with a crisp potato "chip" precariously perched on top; the intensely flavorful bouillabaisse is no less than revelatory. As the name implies, Blackfish's menu focuses heavily on seafood but the Pekin duck with mustard greens and quinoa and the Lancaster County poulard are notable choices.

Costa Deli, 901 E. Butler Pk., Ambler, PA 19002; (215) 646-6173; costadeli.com; Traditional American/Deli; $. Time may continue to march on all around this tiny family-owned deli/luncheonette, but the Costa family remains committed to tradition. For more than 60 years, the old-school staple has been serving up cheesesteaks, hoagies, hot dogs, and sandwiches and their signature milk shakes to hungry loyalists. Though the food is certainly a draw, part of this place's charm is the friendly and warm service. Current manager David Costa, grandson of the original owner, is as likely to offer samples of artisanal cheese as he is to spend some time chatting with you. In the back, there's a small seating area outfitted with bistro-like tables for those wishing to linger over their meals or chat with the affable staff. Costa's also offers an excellent assortment of grocery and specialty items like fresh ravioli, meats, and cheeses. A display case atop the lunch counter houses an array of homemade gourmet cupcakes like chocolate ganache and red velvet. Much to the delight of suburbanites, the deli carries a line of products from **Di Bruno Brothers** (p. 154), making it far easier to enjoy the famed specialty shop's wares without having to venture into the city. See the recipe for **Costa's Original Italian Hoagie** on p. 255.

Jules Thin Crust Pizza, 78 S. Main St., Doylestown, PA 18902; (215) 345-8537; julesthincrust.com; Pizza; $$. Located in the historical district of Doylestown, Jules Thin Crust's is a local outfit specializing in all-organic, natural, thin-crust pizza featuring a variety of meats and assorted accoutrements. All salads are organic as well and are complemented by a selection of homemade dressings like Caesar, balsamic, and a creamy buttermilk ranch. Though the meat-topped pies are delicious, Jules is a veggie lover's delight—the #15 is a tasty mash-up of butternut squash, apples, ricotta and mascarpone cheese, caramelized onions, and mozzarella. In keeping with the something-for-everyone theme, any medium-size pizza can be made gluten-free; a daily selection of comforting homemade soups completes the menu. Don't miss the selection of craft and root sodas.

Majolica, 258 Bridge St., Phoenixville, PA 19460; (610) 917-0962; majolicarestaurant.com; French; $$$. Phoenixville's tagline proclaims that it is "a town worth the trip," which could easily refer to its nearly hour-long distance from Philadelphia. To its credit, the town *is* worth the trip as it is enjoying a revitalization of its town center—quaint little shops and hip restaurants are cropping up all along its main street. There are also a few fine dining selections and among them is French-influenced BYOB Majolica, where Chef-Owner Andrew Deery masterfully creates sultry sauces and incorporates seasonal ingredients into his rotating menu. Small plates like squash blossoms with smoked salmon and a unique black olive oil seemingly melt on the tongue; peekytoe crab and herb salad with a savory, refreshing gazpacho water is light and vibrant. The menu of charcuterie and cheese boards, pastas, flatbreads, and larger plates offers many highlights. For a true indulgence, opt for one of the tasting menus, which feature menu items and the chef's creations. Sunday brunch, which includes a

Over the Hills & through the Woods.

Foodies and local eating enthusiasts looking to get out of the city for a while will enjoy this van tour through the backwoods of Bucks County led by locavores and area experts Alan Brown and Lynne Goldman. Each tour is approximately 5 hours long and offers participants the chance to meet and interact with local purveyors, food artisans, and producers and learn about area establishments from a behind-the-scenes vantage point. The duo offers impressively extensive itineraries like the Mixed Bag of Bucks (an exciting sampler tour that introduces participants to some of the finest food in the area) and the Meat and Greet which, as its name implies, showcases the talents of the county's best butchers. The van ride itself provides a relaxing trip through the idyllic countryside of Bucks County, while the informative lessons on everything from local lore to seasonal produce give more insight to an area whose culinary wonders still remain a mystery to some. The itineraries change frequently and are largely dependent upon growing and production seasons; customizable tours are available as well. It is highly recommended that participants bring along spending cash and an empty cooler to stock up on goodies along the way. **Bucks County Food Tours;** *(215) 794-4191 or (215) 598-3979; buckscountyfoodtours.com.*

complimentary mimosa, presents patrons with yet another opportunity to gain insight to the chef's whims as the menu rotates frequently.

Gilmore's Restaurant, 133 E. Gay St., West Chester, PA 19380; (610) 431-2800; gilmoresrestaurant.com; French; $$$. After a highlight-filled 22 years as Le Bec-Fin's Chef de Cuisine, Peter Gilmore struck out on his own and opened this quaint BYOB nestled in a West Chester town house. The diminutive dining room—though a bit cramped—lends itself to an intimate, conversational dinner. Diners can sip a robust Bordeaux in this beautiful setting while savoring a delightful lobster panna cotta with anisette cream and caviar or the same shrimp mousse–bound *galette de crabe* that made Chef Gilmore's former employer famous. To the uninitiated, duck confit with pear-raisin chutney offers a tasty primer. A 3-course weekday tasting menu is available as well.

Margaret Kuo's, 4-6 W. State St., Media, PA 19063; (610) 892-0115; margaretkuos.com; Japanese; $$. Owner and restaurant namesake Margaret Kuo is often credited with singlehandedly introducing authentic Chinese cuisine to the area's suburbanites; she is also known for beautifully designed interiors in her upscale restaurants. Kuo presides over her four-restaurant dynasty (that includes one fast casual eatery) with a keen eye and has earned a reputation for hiring top talent to helm her restaurants' kitchens. Trained by the prestigious Imperial Kitchen Staff in Tokyo, the chef at Kuo's crown jewel is as adroit at preparing Japanese delicacies like uni tempura and *usu zukuri* (thinly sliced fish) as he is at Peking duck.

Paramour, 139 E. Lancaster Ave., Wayne, PA 19087; (610) 977-0600; paramourwayne.com; New American; $$$$. Located in the posh Wayne Hotel, Paramour boasts a whopping four dining areas including a bistro bar and a formal dining room. Executed by Chef Michael Giampa, the menu offers such innovations as a silken caramelized cauliflower soup with Maine lobster and corn relish and a shaved root vegetable salad. In true something-for-everyone style, the menu is a mix of artisanal flatbreads, salads, small tapas-like plates, larger entrees, steaks, and chops. A limited number of raw bar items and a sampler of crudo supplement the larger menu. Try the crispy duck with quail egg, apple butter, and freshly shaved horseradish or the soulful pork cheeks with creamy grits and a

smattering of onion jam. Sunday brunch is a grand affair with the huge, option-filled Bloody Mary bar taking center stage. Indulge in the eye-opening cocoa waffles with salted caramel ice cream and vanilla syrup, which taste more dessert-like than a traditional waffle. For a savory morning starter, the breakfast sliders—housemade sausage topped with farm-fresh cheddar and a minuscule quail egg—are a sure thing.

Savona, 100 Old Gulph Rd., Gulph Mills, PA 19428; (610) 520-1200; savonarestaurant.com; New American; $$$$. For many, it's hard to justify spending $40 for an entree at a suburban restaurant and, while Savona tends to err on the side of priciness, this white tablecloth eatery consistently turns out a fine menu of dishes focused primarily on the Abruzzo region of Italy. Seared day boat scallops scattered with pignoli, roasted eggplant, and smoky pancetta is a revelatory dish. The restaurant itself is divided into distinct parts with Bar Savona being the more relaxed, casual option of the two. Start with lemon zest-dusted fried artichoke or an heirloom beet and goat cheese salad before delving into a wood-fired *papa grasso*—a thin-crusted braised pork, roasted garlic, broccoli rabe, and sharp provolone pizza. Creamy risotto, an array of freshly made pastas, and heartier entrees make up the rest of the bar's menu. Savona also boasts a wine list of over 1,000 bottles hand-selected by an in-house master sommelier; a creative cocktail list offers an eclectic mix of libations. Indulge your daring side and try the absinthe- and orange-based Bon Vivant.

Sycamore, 14 S. Lansdowne Ave., Lansdowne, PA 19050; (484) 461-2867; sycamorebyo.com; New American; $$$. When Sycamore first opened, it set the culinary world abuzz—thanks in part to its heartthrob chef Sam Jacobson. His adoring Yelp fans (especially females) often wax poetic about his ever-changing menus and farm fresh dishes and he is more than deserving of the praise. Thanks to a relationship with area purveyors, the emphasis at Sycamore is on local and seasonal ingredients, which constantly rotate based on what is available. The succinct menu may include an artisanal cheese or charcuterie plate or the wild mushroom toast with a truffled sunny-side-up egg—a cult favorite. Consider yourself lucky if the New Jersey scallops with chickpea and scallion fritters make an appearance on the menu. Tuesday night offers a prix fixe chef's tasting that changes frequently.

Totaro's Restaurant, 729 E. Hector St., Conshohocken, PA 19428; (610) 828-9341; totaros.com; Italian; $$. Burrowed deep in residential Conshohocken, this local stalwart has been around for more than 50 years. Unsuspecting with its slightly weathered exterior, Totaro's looks like the average tavern from the outside, but there are some pretty above-average things going on inside. Though pricey, much of the menu of reworked classic Italian dishes and a unique offering of game is worth the extra coin. Expect to find venison, elk, or boar gracing the menu from time to time, but look for faithful favorites like chicken saltimbocca and gnocchi Genovese to remain; 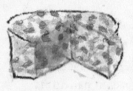 the signature osso buco is a must. If you're looking for something a bit more casual, there's a sports bar of sorts (albeit a little worn) where you can snag chicken wings that come with an addictive house-made blue cheese dressing or, should you feel the need to be adventurous, frog legs. Decadent desserts are made in-house by Totaro's skilled resident pastry chef. Keep an eye out for special dinners and live entertainment.

Zachary's BBQ, 1709 Markley St., Norristown, PA 19401; (610) 272-1800; zacharysbbq.com; Barbecue; $$. Zachary's is a down-home barbecue joint that offers home-style classics culled from age-old family recipes. Thankfully, in contrast to many of the corporate-like barbecue restaurants in the city, this Norristown hotspot is the real deal. Smoked sausage, Texas-style brisket, "pulled" meats, and ribs are the obvious highlights, but a hefty list of traditional sides is a close second. A gooey macaroni and cheese (made with four types of cheeses) may be the natural enemy of your waistline, but it's your palate's best friend. Paired with the smoky meats, Gram's potato salad, hoppin' john, and slightly sweet baked beans are reminiscent of all the elements that make for a good old fashioned backyard 'cue. After chowing down on a plateful of good eats, try a slice of the maple bourbon pecan pie—if you can fathom taking another bite. See Chef Keith Taylor's recipe for **Low Country Jambalaya** on p. 253.

Rocky Road Roadmap: An Ice Cream Lover's Dream

While ice cream shops are plentiful, getting out of the city to explore the surrounding countryside and visit the outlying area's best creameries and ice cream shops makes for not only a scenic road trip but a tasty one as well.

Brown's Cow, 30 S. Main St., Phoenixville, PA 19460; (610) 933-0695; brownscow.com. This Phoenixville favorite serves Bassetts premium ice cream—a Pennsylvania staple that, at over 120 years old, is the nation's oldest ice cream maker. Must-try: Pistachio, Rum Raisin.

Carmen and David's Creamery, 25 N. Prince St., Lancaster, PA 17603; (717) 393-2015; carmenanddavidscreamery.com. David, one half of the ice cream–producing duo, decided the best way to learn about ice cream–making was to go to college (Penn State) and study the cold stuff, and it paid off in spades. C&D's is part of Lancaster's "Buy Fresh Buy Local" initiative, and they believe in using the freshest produce and ingredients available—evident in every delicious spoonful. Flavors here go beyond the traditional and are subject to the whims (and innovation) of the owners themselves. Must-try: Salted Caramel and Lemon Ginger Cookie.

DelVal Creamery, 2100 Lower State Rd., Doylestown, PA 18901; (215) 230-7170; themarketatdelval.com. Delaware Valley College's answer to ice cream prayers, this creamery is operated by Shady Brook Farm and has an impressive list of flavors. The super-premium ice cream is sold inside the Market at DelVal along with fresh produce, local wines, prepared foods, and artisanal jams and preserves. Must-try: Pumpkin (seasonal), Toasted Coconut.

Dilly's Corner, 2998 River Rd., New Hope, PA 18938; (215) 862-5333. Nostalgia and a menu of simple classics like hot dogs, burgers, and fries keep the crowds coming to this Bucks County institution. Dilly's claim to fame—other than great food and ice cream—is its reputation as the place to visit after spending a day rafting or tubing on the Delaware River. Expect long lines at

ICE CREAM UNIVERSITY

Even the staunchest ice cream lovers have a hard time justifying a 4-hour drive from Philadelphia to snag some of the cold stuff, but one taste of a scoop of Berkey Creamery's finest and you'll be convinced. The creamery is named after local couple Jeanne and Earl Berkey—the owners of Berkey Milk Company who eventually transitioned into the ice cream retail business. Over the years, the duo helped many a Penn Stater get started in the dairy industry; eventually their plant was used by the university for milk testing.

Today, the store is more than double the size of the original creamery and has both indoor and outdoor seating where students and visitors alike flock to enjoy cones and dishes filled with enormous scoops of the area's best ice cream, frozen yogurt, and sherbet. The dizzying selection of flavors is a tad overwhelming and though flavor mixing is not allowed, helpful (and patient) staffers are always willing to give the indecisive a sample or two. On most days, there are over 20 available flavors; high points include Chocolate Pretzel Crunch, Happy Happy Joy Joy (an ice cream version of an Almond Joy candy bar), Southern Pecan Cheesecake, and Maple Nut.

Many of the flavors on the list are available in take-home quart and half-gallon sizes, and don't worry if you've trekked to the creamery from far away—insulated bags and inexpensive dry ice are available to keep your sweet treats intact. **Berkey Creamery,** *119 Food Science Building (Pennsylvania State University campus), University Park, PA 16802; (814) 865-7535; creamery.psu.edu* the roadside stand during the summer months, but a simple soft-serve vanilla/chocolate swirl is worth the wait. Must-try: Vanilla/Chocolate Swirl.

Freddy Hill Farms, 1440 Sumneytown Pike, Lansdale, PA 19446; (215) 855-1205; freddyhill.com. An ice cream shop, general store, mini-golf course and a petting zoo all rolled into one, Freddy Hill is a working farm and serves pay-by-weight ice cream at $0.44/oz. Family-friendly events are offered throughout the year; check the website for details. Must-try: Butter Brickle.

Gerenser's Exotic Ice Cream, 22 S. Main St., New Hope, PA 18938; (215) 862-2050. Though quality can be inconsistent at times, cash-only Gerenser's is still a New Hope landmark that offers flashes of brilliance more often than not. The ice cream menu is pretty extensive and presents some nontraditional (though not as exotic as the term would imply) as well as classic flavors. If you're strolling through the quaint town of New Hope, a visit to Gerenser's is a given. Must-try: Nut Salad and Rocky Road.

The Inside Scoop, 301 N. 3rd St., Coopersburg, PA 18036; (610) 282-1955; theinsidescoop.com. Reminiscent of a '50s malt shop with a funky and upgraded decor, The Inside Scoop serves up innovative flavors and monstrous sundaes. During warmer months, the Little League baseball field that shares a parking lot with the ice cream shop draws big crowds and lines can get long—a semi-functioning drive-thru (skip the intercom and drive up to the window instead) is a savior during busy times. Must-try: Maple Bacon and PB&J.

The Last Temptation, 115 S. Main St., Ste. A, New Hope, PA; (215) 862-3219. New Hope has a reputation for being an ice cream lover's paradise and this little charmer, serving ice cream from popular Thomas Sweet, is at the top of the list. Must-try: Salted Caramel.

Longacre's Modern Dairy, 1445 Route 100, Barto, PA 19503; (610) 845-7551; longacresdairy.com. To drive through the small town of Barto is to step back in time, and even though Longacre's calls itself modern, there's an old-school air to the store itself, from its vintage signage to the old-fashioned courtesy of its sweet servers. Sidle up to the lunch counter and order from the menu of retro favorites (including a killer grilled ham and cheese sandwich); a thick milk shake will take you back to the malt shop days. Both hard and soft-serve ice cream varieties are produced at the dairy and distributed to local parlors, stands, and restaurants. Must-try: Peanut Butter Curl.

Merrymead Farm & Country Market, 2222 Valley Forge Rd., Lansdale, PA 19446; (610) 584-4410; merrymead.com. This tucked-away favorite is an expanded general store on a working dairy farm whose ice cream is local legend. Merrymead's country market also sells a variety of produce, jams, candies, and homemade products. The farm hosts fun, interactive seasonal events perfect for families; check the website for a complete schedule. Must-try: Almond Joye (yes, spelled with an "e").

Suloman's Milk Store, 2782 Leidy Rd., Gilbertsville, PA 19525; (610) 323-0314. Suloman's is the tiny outpost general store of an actual working dairy farm (located across the street) where ice cream is made on-premises. Family-owned, service is friendly and helpful; local artisanal foods (pick up a chicken pot pie), milk, butter, and eggs are fresher-than-fresh and are worth the trip. Must-try: Graham Slam.

Living La Vida Local

Fifteen hundred miles. That's the average number of miles a nonlocal meal travels before it makes it to your plate. As the boundaries of our world continue to stretch beyond our own individual communities, food globalization has become a double-edged sword. On one hand, it exposes our palates to a wider variety of food (think star fruit from Indonesia), but on the other hand, the long journey some food has to make—known as "food miles"—poses enough potential problems to make an environmentalist faint. As more and more specialty stores boast organic, artisanal, and local foodstuffs and words like "sustainable" and "locavore" have carved out places in our lexicon, many of us are finally beginning to understand why eating local is so important to our health and our communities.

Philadelphia is fortunate enough to be surrounded by an out-lying countryside of vast farmland, which makes purchasing food that is locally grown and raised from community vendors and farmers that much easier. Community-supported farmers often raise and grow a wider variety of food than is found in the supermarket; anyone who has trolled through the stalls of a farmers' market and mulled over whether to buy an Arkansas Traveler, Bradley, or Jubilee heirloom tomato can testify to that fact.

There are a number of suburban CSAs (community supported agriculture), farmers' markets, and co-ops that support the notion that many local food devotees have long held: The cultivation of fresh, delicious whole foods is essential to a healthy food culture.

Bryn Mawr Farmers' Market (year-round), Municipal Lot 7 on Lancaster Avenue (in front of the Bryn Mawr train station, across from Ludington Library); brynmawrfarmersmarket.blogspot.com. In addition to artisanal chocolates, Philadelphia-roasted coffee, and fresh-cut plants and flowers, eggs and meat from pastured animals, as well as an assortment of produce from local purveyors can be found at this year-round market.

Green Pasture Farms (buying club & traditional CSA), 921 W. Lancaster Ave. Bryn Mawr, PA 19010; greenpasturefarms.com.

Founded by four Pennsylvania families, this buying club/ CSA operates an outpost at the Bryn Mawr Farmers' Market as well as an online buying club. Various foods for sale include pastured meats, artisan cheeses, free-range eggs, 100 percent maple syrup, organic coffee, tea, olive oil, and specialty fudge.

Lancaster County Farmers Market (year-round), 389 W. Lancaster Ave. Wayne, PA 19087; (610) 688-9856; lancastercounty farmersmarket.com. This Wayne farmers' market houses a host of vendors selling a variety of goods—including local produce, poultry, and eggs from nearby Lancaster County.

Lancaster Farm Fresh CSA, lancasterfarmfresh.com. The CSA provides members with 25 weeks of local, certified organic produce from its cooperative network of over 75 Lancaster County family farms; an online buying club as well as community-supported medicine are also available.

Linvilla Orchards (year-round), 137 W. Knowlton Rd., Media, PA 19063; (610) 876-7116; linvilla.com. Anyone who grew up in the tri-state area has taken at least one school field trip to this produce playground; call it a rite of passage for elementary schoolchildren. While tiny tots are drawn to Linvilla for its roster of kid-friendly activities like the famed hayrides, festivals, holiday-themed attractions, and the like, adults bask in the abundance of its grown-on-site produce and stuffed-to-the-rafters farm market that offers irresistible goodies like fresh-baked breads, pizza, cakes, and the famous apple cider doughnuts and pies (which, by the way, come in over 40 varieties). As if that isn't enough, the market boasts an impressive assortment of gourmet specialty items, honey, preserves, cider, milk, eggs, artisanal cheeses, and confections. For those wanting to get closer to their food, there is a seasonal pick-your-own schedule that allows enthusiasts to trek into the orchards and growing fields and snag their own fruits and veggies. If you're itching to test your hand at the rod and reel, Orchard Lake—the on-site fishing hole—is hand-stocked by staff and requires no permit.

The Market at DelVal (year-round), 2100 Lower State Rd., Doylestown, PA 18901; (215) 230-7170; themarketatdelval.com. Managed by Shady Brook Farm, the market boasts a bounty of local produce, Pennsylvania wines and an impressive ice cream counter (p. 218). The market also offers a number of family-friendly activities year-round.

Philadelphia CowShare, phillycowshare.com. Philadelphia CowShare allows individuals to buy high quality, local, grass-fed beef in bulk by splitting the purchase of a cow with other buyers. Several cuts are available and membership can be purchased online.

Swarthmore Co-op (year-round), 341 Dartmouth Ave., Swarthmore, PA 19081; (610) 543-9805; swarthmore.coop. While this 75-year-old institution has a roster of 1,100 members, anyone can shop at the co-op. There are a number of local items available and there are even in-house catering services. Those interested in membership can sign up online or in-store.

Weavers Way Co-op (year-round), 8424 Germantown Ave., Philadelphia, PA 19118; (215) 866-9150; weaversway.coop. This jack-of-all-trades co-op offers an array of services including notary public service, postage sales, and faxing/photocopying capabilities. The grocery store sells a variety of local produce, meats, and dairy at its Mount Airy and Chestnut Hill locations.

Suburban Culinary Classes

Hamanassett B&B, 725 Darlington Rd., Chester Heights, PA 19017; (610) 459-3000; hamanassett.com. Nestled in an upscale residential neighborhood in the Brandywine Valley, Hamanassett is a stately bed and breakfast known just as much for its innate beauty as it is for its renowned cooking school. Cooking enthusiasts have the option of choosing to include a 2-day stay on the property or to participate in the class only. Innkeepers Glenn and Ashley Mon have designed a class schedule that include standouts like a re-creation of a first-class dinner aboard the *Titanic* or learning how to prepare past presidents' favorite meals in what is billed as a mock White House state dinner. Occasionally, classes are taught by local celebrity chefs, but more often than not classically trained chef Ann-Michelle Albertson is at the kitchen's helm teaching participants how to slice, dice, chop, and sauté. After dishes are prepared, students then become diners as they ease into the formal dining room to taste the fruits of their labor. The drawing room is the perfect place to enjoy an after-dinner glass of port and converse with classmates or listen as one of the innkeepers regales the group with spine-tingling paranormal stories about the historic property.

Sur La Table, 690 W. Dekalb Pk., King of Prussia, PA 19406; (484) 612-0046; surlatable.com. It's easy to get distracted by the shiny gadgetry, cutlery, and seemingly endless inventory of cookware at this kitchen giant, but if you can tear yourself away from browsing the aisles, consider taking one of the cooking classes that cover a number of topics. Informative classes tackle subject matters like pasta-making and the sharpening of knife skills. The culinary calendar offers additional classes ranging from introductory ethnic cuisine to French pastry workshops; young cooking enthusiasts can learn their way around the kitchen with one of the kids' cooking classes. Themed offerings like the Girls' Night Out and Date Night series are worth checking out as well.

Viking Culinary Arts Center, 1 Town Pl., Ste. 100, Bryn Mawr, PA 19010; (610) 526-9020; vikingcookingschool.com. Anyone who has ever dreamed of cooking in a kitchen full of sleek appliances, cookware, and cutlery should sign up for one of the Viking culinary classes, where the sophisticated gadgetry rivals the cooking classes themselves. In general, the classes cover subjects such as ethnic and vegetarian cuisines, basic techniques of cooking, baking, and cocktail and dinner parties. There are several locations dotted around the country, with the Pennsylvania culinary arts center offering classes almost daily, ranging from an extensive lesson in fish cookery to a Thai dinner party to a surf-and-turf workshop. There is a class offered for everyone from culinary novices to skillful home cooks and everyone in between; there are even classes for teenagers looking to cultivate their kitchen skills. Classes tend to sell out quickly; check the website and book early.

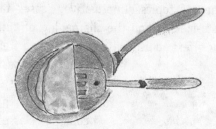

Food Festivals & Events

There's no doubt that the city of Philadelphia is a busy place; the social calendar is always packed with new things to see or try—and, more importantly, eat. Residents have big appetites and a genuine love of food, so many of the events in and around the city are food-centric. Some are charitable and benefit local foundations and causes, some celebrate ethnic cuisine or seasonal bounty, while others are just downright quirky. While the events often attract diverse crowds—from the novice, picky foodie to the gastronome who eats with gusto—one thing remains certain: Philadelphia is a city that knows how to celebrate all things edible.

There seems to always be some type of food festival or neighborhood celebration going on, so for a current list of happenings, contact the **Greater Philadelphia Tourism Marketing Corporation** (visitphilly.com; 215-599-0776) or the **Philadelphia Convention and Visitors Bureau** (philadelphiausa.travel; 800-CALL-PHL or 800-225-5745). Both are excellent resources for current events taking place in the surrounding countryside and outlying suburbs as well.

The following list of events focuses solely on annual events, which are listed in the months in which they usually occur. For specific dates, consult the website listed for individual events.

January

Center City District Restaurant Week and University City Dining Days. January welcomes both of these dining experiences, which focus on offering the city's best eats for less. During the former, which occurs in January and again in September, diners can choose 3-course dinners at over 120 of the city's top eateries for a mere $35 or lunch for $20. Throughout the latter, diners can experience a taste of the eclectic University City dining scene by taking part in a 3-course, 3-price promotion, which allows them to choose from $15, $25, or $30 meals. For Center City, go to centercityphila .org. For University City, go to universitycity.org/diningdays.

Taste Local!, (610) 292-0880; rollingbarrel.com. The city flaunts its love for food and drink as breweries, wineries, and local chefs come together to encourage attendees, as the title implies, to taste local goods. Educational sessions demonstrate interesting food and wine pairings as visitors are invited to sample the bites.

February

Groundhog Day Hawaiian Shirt Beer Breakfast, (215) 856-3591; greylodge.com. Try saying this event's title five times fast, though it may get harder with each beer you consume at Grey Lodge's annual homage to everyone's favorite weather-predicting rodent Punxsutawney Phil. The Frankford Avenue bar opens its doors at 7 a.m. to welcome loyal residents and oddballs alike who faithfully come to celebrate the day and see Grey Lodge's resident lucky cat, Wissinoming Winnie, make her own prediction whether there will be six more weeks of winter, or if spring seasonal beers will come early.

Wing Bowl, (215) 592-0610; 610wip.com. Only the city of Philadelphia would hold a chicken wing eating contest in an arena that has hosted the likes of Bruce Springsteen and U2. Yes, this event, which pits amateur eaters against one another, consistently draws crowds in excess of 20,000 spectators (many of whom camp out a half-day before the event). The gluttonous display is a fun, rowdy contest with local radio DJs, competition judges and quirky personalities showing up to take part. Don't forget to keep your eyes peeled for the "Wingettes"—scantily clad females who cheer on and encourage the participants.

March

Brewer's Plate, (215) 386-5211; fairfood philly.org. Fair Food Philly, an organization that promotes local and sustainable eating, welcomes more than 1,000 attendees to its signature fête normally held at the University of Pennsylvania Museum of Archaeology and Anthropology. The event celebrates beverages and food from the best breweries and restaurants within 150 miles of Philadelphia.

Philly Craft Beer Festival, phillycraftbeerfest.com. This event sells out every year and has been recognized by *Forbes Traveler* as one of the "Top 10 Beer Festivals in America." Over 50 of the nation's top craft breweries set up shop to dole out samples of their finest offerings to eager beer lovers.

Running of the Micks, (215) 574-9317; runningofthemicks.com. At this annual St. Patrick's Day pub crawl, you don't have to be Irish to appreciate the scores of people attired in green or dressed as leprechauns. Dozens of buses transport the green beer–drinking set around town to participating pubs, which host the merry revelers who later make their way to Philadelphia Museum of Art to run up the famous steps.

April

Bucks County Chocolate Show, buckscounty chocolateshow.com. Chocolate enjoys a long and storied history and chocoholics can nosh on artisanal chocolates and learn about the latest trends in chocolate-making and production through various on-site exhibits.

Flavors of the Avenue, (215) 336-1455; visiteastpassyunk.com. East Passyunk in South Philadelphia is being hailed as one of the premier up-and-coming dining destinations. There are an impressive number of hot, new restaurants—many of which serve craft ale.

More than 20 of the neighborhood's most popular restaurants and bars gather to serve up some of the tastiest food in the area while musicians, a fashion show, and a craft market are outside dotted along the avenue.

Friday the Firkenteenth, (215) 825-5357, greylodge.com. Friday the 13th strikes fear in the hearts of the superstitious, but the wise know that the best way to ward off bad luck is to head to Grey Lodge for the all-day event where several firkins (small casks) are tapped and worrywarts can sip cask ale and take their minds off of black cats and all things unlucky. (Actual month varies.)

Strawberry Festival, (215) 794-4000; peddlersvillage.com. In this quaint and charming Bucks County dining and shopping mecca, berry lovers sample the finest that the season's harvest has to offer in the form of jams, preserves, pies, tarts, and cakes.

May

German Bock Festival, (610) 935-4540; slyfoxbeer.com. Who said cat and dog owners have all the fun? On the first Sunday in May, goat owners can bring their horned friends to race other goats in the parking lot of Sly Fox Brewhouse & Eatery in Phoenixville. This race may sound odd to some, but there's a serious prize on the line: the honor of having a maibock named after the owner of the winning goat. Apparently, the competition is stiff—for three years running a three-legged goat named Peggy has gone home victorious. Those who aren't interested in the animal festivities can head inside to partake in what is believed to be the largest pouring of Bock beers at any American brewpub in a single day.

Philadelphia Wine Festival, (215) 279-8313; phillymag .com. Oenophiles congregate at this *Philadelphia* magazine-sponsored event to celebrate and learn about more than 200 rare vintages and blends. Wine tastings coupled with food pairing from some of the city's most notable restaurants make this one of the best-attended gatherings of the year.

South 9th Street Italian Market Festival, (215) 922-1766; italianmarketphilly.org. The usual sounds of the Italian Market are kicked up a notch (or two) with the help of several soundstages of musicians dotted around the neighborhood as hungry festivalgoers nosh on bites from the Italian, Vietnamese, and Mexican market vendors.

June

The Great Chefs Event, (866) 333-1213; alexslemonade.org. Some of the nation's most celebrated chefs come together at this charitable event benefitting Alex's Lemonade Stand Foundation and offer attendees the rare chance to sample food from so many top toques under one roof. In recent years, marquee names like Tom Colicchio, John Besh, Masaharu Morimoto, and Philadelphia's own José Garces graced the list of participating chefs.

Linvilla Orchards, (610) 876-7116; linvilla.com. Each year, fruit and veggie lovers flock to family-friendly Linvilla Orchards to roam the 300-acre farm and sample the bounty of the land. Throughout the harvest season, there are festivals devoted to berries, fruit, and corn—including pick-your-own activities, family games, and hayrides. Make sure you stop by the on-site bakery and pick up one of their famous old-fashioned apple pies.

Philly Beer Week, phillybeerweek.org. Beer lovers rejoice as this "week" (actually 10 days) is devoted solely to celebrating craft beer in the city that was crowned "America's Best Beer Town" by *Gourmet* magazine. Highlights include a sumo wrestling tournament between male and female brewers, a charity dunk tank, a host of other gladiator-like beer-centric games, and—of course—plenty of beer drinking.

A Taste of Philadelphia, (215) 683-2200; americasbirthday .com. Often called the "Cradle of Liberty," there's no better place to celebrate America's birthday than Philadelphia. For foodies, the festivities kick off in the latter part of June at the Great Plaza at Penn's Landing and continue up until the grand finale that culminates in a fireworks-filled Fourth of July celebration. Revelers get a chance to sample fare from some of the finest restaurants in the city and sweets seekers can get their frozen dairy treat fix at the annual Super Scooper All-You-Can-Eat Ice Cream Festival—also held at the Great Plaza.

Taste of the Nation, tasteofthenation.org/Philadelphia. The nationally recognized child hunger organization, Share Our Strength, brings together the city's top chefs and mixologists at the Loews Philadelphia Hotel as they provide samples of food and spirits to attendees. 100 percent of the proceeds from ticket sales benefit Philadelphia children in need.

July

Bastille Day, (215) 236-5111; easternstate.org. Eastern State Penitentiary is probably most famous for its creepy yearly Halloween tours, but every July, it is converted into the Bastille where crowds participate in an actual "storming" of the legendary (now defunct) prison. Each year, a local woman is chosen to portray Marie Antoinette and tosses out more than 2,000 Tastykake Krimpets (a hometown favorite) while shouting a variation of the Queen's most infamous saying, "Let them eat Tastykakes!" Before the main event, attendees can enjoy the street party and partake in a number of Francophile-friendly events; several area restaurants get into the spirit and offer French-themed menus as well.

Brandywine Valley Big Bang BBQ, (866) 390-4367; bvwine trail.com. Serious oenophiles and rib lovers don't often travel in the same social circles, but at this Brandywine Valley hootenanny, worlds collide and a good time is to be had by all as participating wineries offer tastings, vineyard and cellar tours, art exhibitions, and—naturally—outdoor barbecues.

Royal Stumble, (215) 569-9525; noddinghead.com. Proving that ordinary activities can be made into events, Nodding Head Brewery and Restaurant is the site of this annual contest in which a dozen or so breweries compete to see who can most quickly rid themselves of their entire beer supply. Brewers outfit themselves according to theme, which, in past years, has included everything from superheroes to sumo wrestlers.

Vendy Awards, streetvendor.org. The Vendys, as the event is affectionately called, celebrates mobile food truck/vendor culture. Originally started in New York, the event has spread to other cities as well. In Philadelphia, several local food trucks converge on the Piazza at Schmidt's in the trendy territory of Northern Liberties as scores of foodies line up to sample bites from the best mobile vendors in the city. While there is a panel of local celebrity judges, the Peoples' Choice Award is, perhaps, the most anticipated honor.

August

Philadelphia Caribbean Festival, phillycaribbeanfestival.com. The Great Plaza at Penn's Landing is the setting for the festive late-summer event that celebrates the culture, food, and music of 14 Caribbean islands. Steel bands play while visitors partake in family-friendly activities and shop at the marketplace full of island fashions, souvenirs, arts, and crafts. In addition, the festival offers a children's corner, including a re-creation of an African/Caribbean children's village and maypole dancing.

September

Eat Along the Street (E.A.T.S), manayunk.com. Hungry crowds flock to the neighborhood of Manayunk to sample food from well-known area chefs while a celebrity panel noshes on and judges the participating chefs' bites. Outside, attendees can hop in line to get a taste of an eclectic mix of food from the region's best food trucks.

FEASTIVAL, (215) 413-9006; livearts-fringe.org/feastival. Hosted by famed restaurateur Stephen Starr and esteemed local chefs Michael Solomonov and Audrey Claire Taichman, the swank, highly anticipated gala is the banner fundraiser for Philadelphia Live Arts Festival and Philly Fringe. Guests can rub elbows with the region's best-known chefs and sample their dishes, witness art performances, and participate in live and silent auctions.

 Mushroom Festival, (610) 925-3373; mushroomfestival.org. The town of Kennett Square basks in its reputation as the "Mushroom Capital of the World" with a weekend of tastings, cooking demos, cook-offs, and farm tours. There's also a 5K run, a nighttime parade, and a wine-and-soup tasting—all in praise of the versatile fungus.

October

Dining with the Dead, (215) 228-8200; thelaurelhillcemetery .org. Brave souls venture to this North Philadelphia graveyard to commune with the dead and toast to their memories at this bring-your-own-bottle candlelight dinner held appropriately during the month of October.

Philadelphia Food & Wine Festival, (609) 398-4450; gourmet shows.com/philly. The Valley Forge Convention Center hosts one of the largest gatherings of food enthusiasts and wine sippers in the area as celebrity chefs offer cooking demos and food samples. Visitors can also get a sneak peek of the newest culinary products and gadgets in the event's gourmet marketplace.

November

Apple Festival, (215) 794-4000; peddlers village.com. City dwellers can break out of their concrete surroundings and take a trip to the charming little shopping and dining town of Peddler's Village for this 2-day festival. The humble apple is  celebrated with a bounty of apple-centric treats like fritters, apple butter, cider, and dumplings. Live musicians, a juried craft show, and messy pie-eating contests round out the weekend's activities.

Christmas Village, philachristmas.com. From Thanksgiving to Christmas Eve, more than 400,000 people visit Love Park during this open-air gathering of local merchants. Modeled after the traditional Christmas markets of Germany, vendors set up shop in more than 50 wooden booths to sell traditional European food, beverages, and sweet treats. Shoppers can also get some Christmas gift-buying done as many vendors offer international holiday gifts, ornaments, jewelry, and high-end arts and crafts.

Nouveau Release, buckscountywinetrail.com. The arrival of the French wine known as Beaujolais Nouveau, harvested in September and shipped in November, is celebrated all over the world, and this Bucks County event offers visitors not only a taste of the famed wine but also the year's newest releases.

December

The Running of the Santas, runningofthesantas.com. When nearly 6,000 twenty-somethings gather in the street, it's usually cause for concern, but this jovial event is just harmless fun. This pub crawl of sorts features tipsy youngsters dressed as good ol' St. Nick as they engage in a footrace in an attempt to reach the next pub first.

Recipes

Philadelphia is home to a number of chefs and culinary professionals who appreciate the city's geographic proximity to a countryside teeming with farmland and bountiful crops. One look at a restaurant's menu often reveals the chef's passion for using farm-fresh ingredients and may inspire you to concoct your own culinary delights. The following recipes have been retooled for the home cook but are no less delicious than their restaurant versions. Special thanks to the chefs, caterers, and shop owners who generously shared their time and recipes.

Stuffed Bell Peppers

Michael Scipione of Sano Catering is a chef on a mission. Self-taught and determined to prove that healthy food can be as delicious—if not more so—than its fattening alternatives, he works as a private chef in Philadelphia and can be seen at many local food events and his gym, Absolute Definition.

Makes 6 stuffed peppers

- 2 tablespoons olive or canola oil
- 1 pound low-fat turkey sausage (remove casing)
- ¾ pound shallots, chopped
- ½ teaspoon sea salt
- ¾ teaspoon coarse ground black pepper
- 1 teaspoon crushed red pepper
- 1 large head broccoli rabe, cleaned, stemmed, and chopped
- Zest of 1 lemon
- ¼ cup white balsamic vinegar

- 1 cup Pinot Grigio (optional)
- 2 (28-ounce) cans crushed tomatoes
- 3 cups chicken stock (low fat/low sodium), divided
- 1 cup heart-healthy pecorino cheese
- 1 16 oz. box instant whole-grain brown rice (cooked accordings to package directions)
- 6 bell peppers, halved lengthwise
- Food processor or blender

Note: *To make this a vegetarian meal, substitute white beans for turkey sausage, and veggie stock instead of chicken.*

In a large pan on high flame add 2 tablespoons of olive oil. Add the turkey sausage (with casings removed).

Chop turkey sausage with spatula as it browns. Then add the shallots, salt, black pepper, and red pepper while still chopping the mixture, until the shallots start to turn translucent.

Add the broccoli rabe and, as it wilts, begin to stir. When the rabe is incorporated and the liquid has evaporated, add lemon zest and then the white balsamic vinegar to deglaze.

Once the vinegar smell dissipates, add the wine, if using. When the alcohol smell dissipates, add the crushed tomatoes and 2 cups chicken stock. Reduce until almost all the liquid has evaporated.

In a food processor or blender, add the cooked ingredients along with the cheese (you may have to process in two batches, depending on the size of the processor).

In a large bowl, add this mixture to the already cooked brown rice, mixing thoroughly to coat all of the rice.

With a large spoon, stuff the mixture into the cleaned, halved, and deveined bell peppers and place the peppers stuffing side up in two large pots.

Fill the pots with the remainder of the sauce plus 1 cup of the stock, about halfway up the side of the peppers (do not submerge the peppers). Spoon additional sauce over the top of the peppers; the peppers will season the sauce.

Bring to a boil and then reduce to simmer with the lid on for 30 to 40 minutes, or until the peppers are fork tender.

Remove the peppers from pots; plate and ladle the reduced sauce over the top.

Courtesy of Chef Michael Scipione of Sano Catering (856-46-8705; livethesanolifestyle.com)

Heirloom Spoonbread

As a self-proclaimed culinary historian and vintage cookbook collector, Chef Al Paris of Heirloom Fine American Cookery delights in reviving classic American recipes and cooking traditions that might have otherwise been lost. While this traditional spoonbread is perfectly delicious eaten on its own, it is at its best served over gumbo or stew.

Serves 4

1 cup cream	1 diced red pepper
1 cup milk	1 diced green pepper
¾ cup cornmeal	3 eggs, separated
3 ounces sharp white cheddar	Pinch of cream of tartar
1 tablespoon salt	

Bring cream and milk to a soft simmer. Fold in remaining ingredients (except egg yolks, egg whites, and cream of tartar); cook over low heat 10 minutes. Remove from heat and let cool for approximately 15 minutes.

Once the mixture has cooled, stir in 3 egg yolks; set aside. Whip 3 egg whites with cream of tartar till stiff peaks form. Fold into cooled mixture.

Pour into a buttered 9x5-inch loaf pan. Bake at 325°F for 30 minutes. Serve by itself or with gumbo or stew.

Courtesy of Chef Al Paris of Heirloom Fine American Cookery (p. 37)

Thai Egg Custard

Chef Moon Krapugthong is a powerhouse and talent whose passion for authentic Thai cooking has injected new vigor into the Manayunk dining scene. This real-deal egg custard dessert is simple in its preparation but complex in its flavor.

Serves 4

1 cup yellow mung beans	**1 cup coconut milk**
4 large eggs	**½ cup thinly sliced shallots**
¾ cup palm sugar	**⅓ cup vegetable oil**

Soak yellow mung beans in water for at least an hour, drain, and then steam until cooked through. Set aside until cooled, approximately 30 minutes.

Preheat oven to 350°F.

Mix the eggs with sugar and beat until creamy. Gradually add coconut milk. After mixing and beating the eggs, sugar, and coconut milk, use a cheesecloth to filter the mixture.

In a saucepan over medium heat, panfry shallots in vegetable oil; stir until they turn brown and crispy. Remove shallots and set aside, but leave excess oil in the pan.

Pour egg mixture and cooked mung beans into the saucepan that already has shallot oil in it. Stir at medium heat until thickened.

Transfer egg mixture from the saucepan to an 8x8-inch ungreased baking pan and spread out with a spatula until about 1 inch thick.

Bake for an hour (keep an eye on custard top as it turns golden brown, but do not allow it to turn dark brown).

Remove from oven and let cool; cut into 2½-inch squares and serve cold.

Note: *For an intoxicating aroma, use a pandan leaf while beating or mixing egg and sugar; take the leaf out after mixing.*

Courtesy of Chef Moon Krapugthong of Chabaa Thai Bistro (p. 31)

Sizzling Mussels

This fresh, simply prepared dish is one of Chef Katz's most popular and is perfect for sharing.

Serves 2

2 dozen cleaned mussels
2 tablespoons white wine
2 tablespoons of Wondra flour
2 tablespoons vegetable oil
Coarse sea salt
Freshly ground black pepper

2 sprigs fresh thyme
1 tablespoon fresh chopped parsley
2 teaspoons fresh lemon juice
Drizzle of extra virgin olive oil
1 cast-iron skillet

Place cleaned mussels with white wine in a sauce pot. Cover and steam over medium heat until mussels just open.

Strain and let sit until cooled. Pick mussels out of shells and discard shells.

Place mussels into mixing bowl. Coat mussels with flour. Shake bowl to coat evenly.

Simultaneously place the cast-iron skillet on a flame to warm and place a medium-size frying pan on high heat. Add vegetable oil to the medium-size frying pan.

When frying pan starts to smoke, add the mussels. Sauté mussels for 3 minutes, continually keeping them moving.

Season with salt and pepper; add thyme and parsley and sauté for 30 seconds. Add one teaspoon of lemon juice to the pan. Toss lightly then place mussels into hot cast-iron skillet. Mussels should sizzle.

To finish, add remaining teaspoon of lemon juice to skillet, drizzle with extra virgin olive oil, sprinkle with sea salt, and serve immediately.

Courtesy of Chef David Katz of Mémé Restaurant (p. 84)

Huarache de Hongos
(Mushroom Flatbread)

This recipe from Xochitl is a bit involved, but it is well worth the effort. One of the most popular appetizers on Xochitl's menu, this flavorful, earthy dish is not only delicious but 100 percent gluten-free.

Serves 2–4

For the Flatbread

4 oz. Maseca (corn masa flour)
1 tablespoon salt

2–3 cups water

Mix all ingredients together until well incorporated and moist, adding more water if necessary until mixture forms a dough ball. Press and form into flat 6-by-4 inch shape with a ¼-inch thickness. In a hot ungreased pan, cook huarache for 2 to 3 minutes per side until browned.

For the Mushroom Filling

2 large portobello mushrooms
Extra virgin olive oil
Salt and pepper to taste
2 oyster mushrooms
Sprig of fresh thyme
1 artichoke, cleaned and
    trimmed down to the heart
    with choke removed

Pinch of red pepper flakes
Lime wedge
3 oz. manchego cheese
1 tablespoon each Cotija
    cheese, chives, and cilantro
    (optional)

Stem and remove gills from portobellos, season, and drizzle with extra virgin olive oil. Roast in a 350°-oven until tender.

Slice portobellos to ¼-inch thickness and set aside.

Remove petals from oyster mushrooms and sear them with thyme in the same pan used for the portobellos. (The pan should still be oiled from the cooking of the portobellos.) Season well with salt and pepper.

Combine sliced portobellos and seared oyster mushrooms.

Heat 1 tablespoon of extra virgin olive oil in a pan over medium heat. Slice artichoke to ⅛-inch thickness and place in hot pan to lightly sear. Remove from heat and add pinch of red pepper flakes, squeeze of lime juice, and extra virgin olive oil.

To Assemble the Flatbread

In a hot pan, heat artichokes and mushrooms and season with salt and pepper.

Sprinkle some manchego on the flatbread lightly and place the mushroom and artichoke mixture on top. Add a small amount of manchego on top and place in the oven just long enough to melt the cheese, approximately 2 minutes.

Remove from oven and cut in half, then cut the halves in half. Garnish with Cotija cheese, chive batons, olive oil, and cilantro (optional).

Courtesy of Chef Gabriel Montalvo of Xochitl (p. 100)

Peach Cobbler with Sugar Cookie Crust

Serves 6–8

For Peach Filling

12 ripe peaches, peeled
2 tablespoons nutmeg
2 tablespoons cinnamon
1½ cups sugar

2 tablespoons vanilla
1 tablespoon lemon juice
1 teaspoon salt

Slice peaches to ¼-inch thickness, combine with all remaining ingredients, and mix well; refrigerate until you finish making crust.

For Sugar Cookie Crust

1 pound butter, softened
1 cup granulated sugar
1 cup powdered sugar

2 tablespoons vanilla
1 teaspoon salt
1½ cups flour

In an electric mixer, cream softened butter and add granulated and powdered sugars. On low speed, mix until well incorporated and add vanilla, salt, and flour and continue to mix well. (The dough should begin to feel like cookie dough.)

Place peach mixture in 8x11-inch baking pan and cover peach mixture completely with dough.

Bake in preheated 350°F oven for 35–40 minutes or until crust is golden brown.

Courtesy of Chef Terrance Clarke of Ms. Tootsie's Soul Food (p. 87)

Low Country Jambalaya

Reaching back into his family's age-old recipes and giving a nod to Southern tradition, Chef Keith Taylor prides himself on his authentic, homey comfort food. Though this jambalaya takes less time than the usual "low and slow" version, it's no less flavorful.

Serves 6–8

- 1 clove garlic, peeled and sliced (omit garlic if using filetto di pomodoro)
- 2 tablespoons blended oil (a blend of 90 percent vegetable oil and 10 percent virgin olive oil; or, if not readily available, substitute vegetable oil)
- 3-4 oz. of smoked andouille sausage (bias cut into approximately ¼-inch thick slices)
- 1 3-5 oz. boneless, skinless chicken breast or boneless thigh meat diced or cut into ½-inch pieces
- 5 large shrimp, peeled and deveined (16/20 count; leave tail on if desired)
- 1 cup holy trinity (medium-diced celery, bell pepper, and onion)
- 1 pinch crushed red chile flakes
- 1 teaspoon fresh oregano
- 1 teaspoon fresh thyme
- 1 teaspoon fresh basil, chopped
- 1 pinch ground cayenne pepper
- ¾ cup fresh seafood or clam stock, or chicken stock
- ¾ cup filetto di pomodoro (a tomato-based "mother" or core sauce) or fresh tomato sauce (refrain from using any tomato sauce that contains cheese and/or meat)
- 1½ cups cooked long-grain rice (preferably Carolina long-grain rice)

1 tablespoon fresh Italian flat-leaf parsley, chopped

1 tablespoon fresh cilantro, chopped

1 tablespoon green onion, chopped, plus extra for garnish

1 teaspoon K. Taylor SIGNATURE Seafood Voodoo spice (or Cajun seasoning)

In a large pan over medium heat, caramelize garlic in blended oil.

In the same pan, sear andouille sausage, chicken, and shrimp. Add trinity and crushed red chile.

Toss in herbs (reserving parsley, cilantro, and green onion) and cayenne pepper, then add stock, tomato sauce, and rice.

Cook until all liquid is absorbed and no longer soupy (be sure to scrape up any caramelized bits that may have stuck to pan); toss in parsley, cilantro, and green onion and stir until incorporated.

Plate in large bowl and top with green onion; sprinkle generously with K. Taylor SIGNATURE Seafood Voodoo spice (or Cajun seasoning).

Courtesy of Chef-Owner Keith Taylor of Zachary's BBQ (p. 216)

Costa's Original Italian Hoagie

In business since 1950, Costa Deli has long been the suburban destination for authentic deli fare. Besides being a place where you can still get an old-school milk shake, cheesesteak, or a Texas Tommy, the Ambler deli lays claim to being the originator of the hoagie that has become one of its most popular items—the Costa's Original Italian Hoagie. The Original Italian Hoagie is different from the standard Italian hoagie, which contains Genoa salami and ham capicola. Founder Rocco Costa—grandfather of the current owner—came up with the recipe decades ago and hungry sandwich lovers still clamor for it.

Serves 1–2

- 1 fresh, good-quality Italian roll (Costa's sources its bread from local favorite Conshohocken Italian Bakery)*
- 3 slices provolone cheese
- 6 slices capicola (not ham capicola)
- 6 slices sopressata
- Shredded lettuce
- 3 tomato slices
- Sliced raw onion
- Pinch of salt and pepper
- Dash of dried oregano
- Good-quality olive oil

*Conshohocken Italian Bakery is located at 79-83 Jones St., Conshohocken, PA 19428 (610-825-9334), and the breads are widely available at vendors throughout the Philadelphia area.

With a sharp knife, make a slit in the bread (be careful not to cut all the way through) and create a hinge. Start assembling the sandwich by arranging the slice of provolone first then follow with the sliced meat. Top with lettuce, tomato, and onion and finish with salt, pepper, oregano, and a drizzle of olive oil.

Recipe courtesy of Owner-Manager David Costa of Costa Deli (p. 209)

Appendix: Eateries by Cuisine

Index